what others

dad while I was a child and as a man. May Hashem bless this work as a wonderful interfaith bridge as well."
Rabbi Steven Berkowitz
Bremerton, WA

"Ed has shared this material in our church over the last 10 years — and it works! I have seen our men come alive as they experienced the love of their father while other men spoke 'the blessing' over their lives. This has taught our men to move from the heart in speaking 'the blessing' over the hearts of their sons and daughters. I have four adult children, and, without a doubt, Ed has shown me and our church what a difference a father makes."
Jeff Newman
pastor, Austin, TX

"Finally! A book that provides a true tangible blessing for you and your children that will change your family relationships forever!"
David A. Wheeler
president of Majestic Realty Co., Los Angeles, CA

"From a child to a teenager. From a teenager to a man. What more could a son ask for? Thanks, Dad, for making a difference. I'm ready!"
Edward Elijah Tandy McGlasson IV
Ed Tandy McGlasson's son

The Difference a Father Makes

calling out the magnificent destiny in your children

Ed Tandy McGlasson

ampelōn
PUBLISHING

Atlanta, GA, USA

Hardback ISBN: 978-0-9748825-2-9
Softcover ISBN: 978-0-9786394-5-7

Printed in the United States of America
Fourth printing

Requests for information should be addressed to:
Ampelon Publishing
6920 Jimmy Carter Blvd., Suite 200
Norcross, GA 30071
To order other Ampelon Publishing products, visit us on the web at:
www.ampelonpublishing.com

To my stepfather, Capt. Daniel E. McGlasson, who called me out to become the father that I am today, and to my departed mother, Jeanne, who was my greatest fan

Contents

Acknowledgements

I want to thank Dr. Rob Johnson for the difference his friendship has made in my life. I cannot count how many hours you have listened, supported, asked questions, and pushed me to follow my dream. Your gift as a writer and editor has made this football player's manuscript readable.

To Brian Holloway whose friendship and inspiration for the last 30 years has given me the courage to go for it and make a difference. He has the ability to make you believe you can change the world. To have him as a friend after all these years is one of my greatest joys.

I am so grateful to my wife, Jill, whose loving touch and consistent support has made the writing of this book possible. She is my friend, wife, counselor, and lover these past 21 years.

To my incredible children Edward, Jessica, Mary Lee, Lukas, and Joshua, who have loved me through the journey of becoming a father. There is nothing in life that comes close to the feeling I get when you let me know that I have made a difference in your life.

To my California family who has always been there, the Andersens, Nelsons, Andrews, and Nanny and Ole.

To east coast family in Maryland who grew up with me the "Navy way." I love you, Cindy, Chan, and Daniel.

To my Aunt Barbara, and cousins, Maurice, Nina, Nanette, Walter, and Chris — you are in my heart.

To my amigo men's group who sacrificially supported me in becoming the man I am today. Their consistent prayer, wisdom, and truth when I have needed it has made the difference for me. There is not a lot of places where you find friends for life. Thanks Dave, Ron, and Rob.

To Jason Chatraw, who, after coming to one of my conferences in Atlanta, relentlessly pursued me until this book was written. Your ability as a writer, editor, and publisher has made this project a joy. And special thanks to Margaret Chatraw, who spent hours poring over these words in editing.

To my church, the Stadium Vineyard, there is not enough room to write all of the names of those who have loved me into the pastor I am becoming.

To my team at the Stadium Vineyard, to Ellen for your work on the manuscript and your friendship, to Glenn whose has always been there to encourage and support me. To Jonathan Rue, a great preacher and communicator in the making, whose fire to serve God and his willingness to do whatever it takes has inspired me.

One final note

A wonderful thing just happened to me as I finished this book. My wife, Jill, decided it was time to find my father's side of the family, which I lost touched with when my father died. She took a day of our vacation and found my father's family, "The Chappellets." Their loving embrace of their cousin has touched me forever. Bless you, Donn and Molly, Lygia and Carlos, Cyril and Blakesley, Jon-Mark and Colleen, Dominic and Sara, Alex and JP, and Carissa, my cousin ambassador at large.

Foreword

You could feel the heaviness in the locker room. Howie Long was sitting silently; Marcus Allen was packing up his travel bag; Bo Jackson was chewing on sun-flower seeds. Frustration was so thick and the pain so real, no one was speaking. John Elway's Broncos had played us tough.

The Raiders never had a losing season like this, ever. I knew I would soon walk off the field forever. The last eight years in the NFL were grueling, and the bone-crushing cold of my years with the New England Patriots had taken their toll. Now, everything hurt. The X-rays revealed a broken finger; surgery was scheduled for the next day.

As I traveled down Highway 101 toward Long Beach, I probably should have been thinking more about our next opponent, but all I could think about was finding Ed.

Somewhere up and down this road in Orange County was my dearest friend. I just had to talk to him. I could not remember his address; I lost his phone number. The pain killers and anti-inflammatory drugs clouded my thinking. I was at a point in my life when the problems, adversity, and heaviness of life started closing in on me. As a man, I really did not have many people I could talk to, men that I trusted.

But Ed always knew just the right thing to say. He made everything seem easier, or maybe I just wanted to hear him laugh again. All I knew was that I had to find him. Once you meet Ed, you have known him for life. I had so much I wanted to say, but I didn't know if any words would actually come out. I would probably just collapse in his arms. I trusted Ed. — *Brian Holloway, 1988*

Right now, you are holding a treasure called *The Difference a Father Makes*. This book will unleash the power, excitement and ferociousness that God intends for us, as men, to go and "take the land," living our lives boldly and courageously. This book will also touch that place in a man that needs to "feel," to hold tenderly and to weep the great tears that only real men can weep.

I've known Ed for almost 30 years, and he has taught me so much about being a man of God, a husband and a father. Ed is a rock, a man who pursues the heart of God.

I knew the NFL could not keep him long — God had bigger plans for him. His wisdom is beyond his years with a message for men, leaders, and families who are ready to go to the next level.

If you happen to be at that place in your life as a husband and father where you are crying out for help, you are at the right place. Whether you had a father in your life, you are in the right place. Ed has spent the last 20 years of his life in the most courageous and exciting journey of all — getting to know God's heart. This book will help you begin a special transformation that takes you from success to significance — that special time in your life where God is calling you forward to move from "what you do" to "what you are for."

When you have finished *The Difference a Father Makes*, please make sure you pass the book along to a friend, maybe even to your father — or to your son. You'll be glad you did.

Brian Holloway
All-Pro NFL tackle & motivational speaker

Looking Toward the Stands

While speaking recently to a group of football players at a local high school, I asked one of the young athletes, "When you're on the field, do you ever look up into the stands?"

"Yes," he responded.

I asked him, "Who are you looking for? And why?"

"I look for my dad," he said. "I am looking for whether or not he is smiling."

"What does that feel like to see him smiling over you?" I asked him.

"There is nothing in my life that means more to me than what my dad thinks of me," he said. "When my dad is there watching, there is nothing I can't do!"

When you are on the field of life, who are you looking for in the stands?

While playing in the city baseball championship, my 11-year-old son, Luke, struck out in his first at-bat of the game. He put his head down and sulked as he walked back to the dugout. Looking for my reaction, he peeked out from underneath his cap, glancing in my direction. I raised my arms in victory and shouted, "You are a champion, son! You are going to blast the next one!" His countenance changed from a frown to a smile. In his next at-bat, he smacked the first pitch against the center field fence. As he rounded second base, he raised his hands and gave me the victory sign. He caught my smile over his life, and his face reflected the love I have for him.

> Do dads understand the power they have been given to make a difference in their kids' lives?

Oftentimes, Little League stands are full of moms but devoid of dads. Where are the fathers? That is the reality that haunts so many young people I meet. Do dads understand the power they have been given to make a difference in their kids' lives?

What was your dad like? Did he have his head down, shaking it in disappointment whenever you couldn't make the big play? Did you even have a dad there? Or was he the one rooting for you, no matter what you did?

If you're a dad today, which one are you?

An involved father can make all the difference in a child's life. His love and care can be the deciding factor in helping a young one become who he or she was created to be. When our hearts are filled with security and trust in a dad who loves us, we stop living *for* our father's approval, and begin to live *from* his approval. Out of our assurance of his unending love and commitment, we're enabled to become the person we were created to be and, in the process, bring pleasure to our dad.

If you are thinking, "I have no idea what that's like" or "My father has never approved of anything I have done," you're not alone. And if you are thinking, "That's not how I am with my son or daughter," it's not too late.

I recently received a letter from a man who attended one of my "The Difference a Father Makes" conferences. I remember him coming up to me with tears in his eyes and asking if it was too late for him to make a difference in his daughter's life? "No," I told him. "It is never too late on this side of heaven to make a difference."

This young father went on. "I am going to go home and do the same thing you did with your daughter."

"Go for it, dad!" I said.

Two weeks later he wrote me these words:

My daughter is 17 and will be attending college this fall. My heart was smitten so much when you shared the experience you had with your daughter that I did almost the exact same thing. I purchased a nice diamond ring for her and asked her to go to dinner with me the night before my next business trip. She was surprised, yet anxious, about the dinner; I believe because I had been traveling so much she thought I just wanted to spend some time with her. I took her out to her favorite restaurant. When we were seated and had ordered our meal, she asked, "So, what did I do?" I told her the reason I wanted to have this time with her was to let her know how much I love her and how proud I am of her.

She and I had to take some deep breaths at that time as we both had tears in our eyes. I then continued, struggling to get the words out about the many assets and accomplishments of hers that I was so proud of. Then I stood up and got down on one knee and pulled out the ring. When she saw it, I must say her expression was that of pure joy. As she began to cry, I looked her in the eyes and said, "I would like to ask you if you would enter into a promise covenant with me, and accept this ring as a token of our covenant. This ring will be given to the man that you and I agree before God is worthy to receive it on your wedding night. Today, I call you to be a woman, and I will treat you as one from this day forward."

She was so excited; we both hugged and tried to hold back the tears, but I really didn't care who was around because, at that moment, nothing else mattered. We are now reading a book together and are excited about what God has in store for us.

Understanding the goal line

One of the biggest problems children face in our culture is that they have no idea when they reach the goal line and become a man or a woman. Was that goal line ever defined for you? When is the day that a little boy arrives at manhood and stops striving to prove himself? How does a little girl cross over into the life of being a woman?

These are all questions we must answer if we are to be fathers who help our children be all they were created to be. This book is about unleashing the incredible power God puts in us, as men, to make a difference by calling out this next generation of men and women who will become our future leaders.

When a local businessman recently came by my office, he looked at me and said, "Ed, the biggest struggle in my life is learning how to deal with my teenage son. He does and says things that make me want to rip his head off. I find myself battling with a lot of anger. I blurt things out that crush him. I find myself doing the same things that my father did to me. I so much want to be a father who calls out the greatness that I know is in my son. But I don't know how to do it." While many men desire to be the kind of father who breathes life into their kids' lives, they've never been given a road map for how to fulfill that desired role.

In the following pages, I want to take you on a journey of discovery, where we uncover the hidden treasures of what it means to be a father who makes a difference in the lives of his children. Our discussion will be frank and heartfelt, challenging you to be the dad perhaps you yourself never had. And even if you never had a father, I will show you how to connect with the greatest Father of all time and to live your life under His smile.

I was determined from the writing of the first page

of this book not only to share my journey, but to answer the "Yeah, but how do I do it?" question.

I remember the first day of training camp when I was drafted by the New York Jets football team. The coaching staff handed each of us a six-inch thick playbook, filled with hundreds of football plays. When head coach Walt Michaels stood up to make his opening speech, he held up the playbook and said, "Men, it is your responsibility to learn these plays. I am not going to hold your hand and make you study this, but there is one thing that will keep you from making this team." Then he said something I have never forgotten.

He said, "If you don't know what you are doing when you are on the field, you will keep the rest of this team from winning, and you will never fulfill your dream of playing in the National Football League."

Most of the young fathers I meet want to make a difference, but they don't know how. In so many of their stories, their own father's blessing was missing. How can a son who has never had his father bless him give a blessing to his kids? We are going to walk through that question together.

I have included a playbook at the back of this book that will teach you the impact positive affirmation, public blessing, shared rituals and values, quality time, built-in structure, and consistent celebration will have on the lives of your kids or those you are mentoring.

My hope is that this book leaves you a changed man with a changed family.

CHAPTER ONE

The Difference
in My Life

Life as a U.S. Navy test pilot was an adventure for my dad, Lt. Ed Tandy. Racing through the sky at speeds of over 600 miles per hour in his Fury Three fighter jet, Lt. Tandy determined whether these planes were fit for their designed purpose. But on one fateful day in 1956, he had to determine much more than that — and he only had seconds to do so.

Tandy's mission was to test the often-faulty oxygen system, which he discovered was still defective. While performing high altitude maneuvers, Tandy began to lose consciousness. His plane began an out-of-control descent toward a California beach packed with people enjoying the sun.

As he raced toward the ground, Tandy recovered consciousness and immediately faced the biggest decision of his life — either bail out and save himself, allowing the plane to crash onto the crowded Monterey Bay beach; or fly the plane into the water to spare those on the beach. With a young bride who was pregnant with their first child, the decision was anything but easy. Yet Tandy had already made his decision the previous evening while reading his Bible.

"Come"

Opening his Bible on the evening prior to his test flight, Tandy began reading the story of Jesus walking on the water in Matthew 14. As he pored over the passage, one word seemed to stand out to him.

> *Peter said to [Jesus], "Lord, if it is You, command me to come to You on the water." And He said, "Come!" And Peter got out of the boat, and walked on the water and came toward Jesus.*
> *— Matthew 14:28-29*

He circled with his red pen the word "come." Something in that word so gripped Tandy that his countenance suddenly changed. His wife saw the look on his face and asked, "Ed, am I going to lose you?" Tandy replied, "No. Why would you say that?" She asked only because she detected a certain unfamiliar look in his eyes.

That night, God spoke to Lt. Ed Tandy about the importance of following His voice. Less than 24 hours later, Tandy heard God's voice loud and clear.

To some of the people sunning on Monterey Bay beach, Tandy's out-of-control airplane must have looked like some special air show. But to a waiting young bride, pregnant with their firstborn son, it was no show at all. It was a day that would change her life — and the life of her son — forever.

In the split second he had to decide, Lt. Tandy made the decision to veer away from the beach and into the water, flying his fighter plane into glory. An eyewitness reported that the plane started to make a recovery from the crash dive, but when the plane ran out of altitude, it suddenly dove straight into the water.

A single word from his Father in heaven gave him the courage to face his destiny. On the eve of Memorial Day in 1956, a hero was welcomed into heaven.

Knowing the kind of man my father was, my mom told me she believed that Ed heard the same word he had circled the night before, answering the call to come.

Where are the fathers?

We can look around and see the devastating aftermath in both families and societies where children are raised without involved and effective fathers. We are given a tremendous responsibility to help usher our children into the destiny God has for them, although we may struggle with the practicalities of how to accomplish that goal.

My dad's death before I was born could have triggered a cycle in which my young life spiraled out of control. Like me, you may not have even known your dad. Or you may have known him as an alcoholic or an abuser. Maybe you only knew him on weekends as a result of a broken home life. Or perhaps your dad lived in your house your whole life, but wasn't there emotionally.

Regardless of your situation, there is still hope — because you have a heavenly Father who will always and forever outshine your earthly father, no matter how great he might be. It was my heavenly Father who spoke to me and explained that the last word on my father's mind before he died — "come" — was the same word He wanted me to use as an invitation to others to know Him. And it was my heavenly Father who placed His loving arms around my life and helped me find my identity in Him.

You may not yet fully grasp the power you have as a father to influence the lives of your children because you never had it modeled in your own life. However, God gives you a tremendous responsibility as a man to help guide your children into the destiny that He has for them. And since God is a good and loving Father, He has placed inside of you the tools you need to call your children into their destiny.

How do I know when I've arrived?

I was fortunate to have a stepdad who loved me as if I was his own. Through his guidance and leadership, I knew the point in my life when I became a man. That knowledge gave me both the courage and the trust to go out and seek my dreams. It also enabled me to grow into a generative father in my own right.

When I read the book, *Wild at Heart* by John Eldridge, he framed a question that has stayed with me: "Even if he can't quite put it into words, every man is haunted by the question, 'Am I really a man? Have I got what it takes ... when it counts?'" That is a big question every young person struggles with. Perhaps even more pressing is this question: How do I know when I have arrived? When does a boy become a man? When does a girl become a woman? And how do they know it?

If you are asking yourself these questions, you're not alone. Most fathers in our culture today have no idea how to call out their children into adulthood because they've had no role model. Jewish tradition has a rite of passage which marks the day a boy enters into manhood — the bar mitzvah. But most Americans in the 21st century have no such ritual.

When was the moment you knew you no longer had to work for the love and approval of your dad? If you haven't experienced such a moment, when will you feel sufficiently secure that you can spend the rest of your life living out your dreams? When will you be able to stop striving for affection and acceptance from your dad or others around you?

Is that really possible?

It is difficult to know what your father thinks about you if you never see him. We have a growing epidemic in our country of fatherless homes. Dr. Scott Larson, president of a ministry designed at reaching juvenile teenagers, found that 50 percent of the children in America go to bed on any given night without the voice of a father in their home. I have come to understand that the question little boys and little girls — as well as men and women — want answered is this: What does my dad really think about me? If that remains a serious question in our lives, we will spend our lives performing for an audience of one man who either doesn't get it or doesn't realize that it's his voice that matters.

Setting the direction for your kids

So, who is setting the direction for the lives of your children? Who is telling them who they are? Who is helping them find their way? If you aren't, someone will be filling your shoes. Is the television telling them how to live their lives? The culture? Their friends?

In a recent survey, Josh McDowell found that 70 percent of teens in his ministry said the number one value in their lives is a sense of family. Why do you think there has been a boom in coffee shops like Starbucks around the world? Because that is the place where kids go to try to find out who they are. They sit and listen to each other's stories. They place tremendous value in hanging out and building relationship, partly because that is not happening at home. Dads have spent their lives building their careers, unaware of what kids want today. Kids don't want bigger houses, faster cars, or more money in the bank. What they really want to know is this: What does my dad really think about me?

> Kids don't want bigger houses, faster cars, or more money in the bank.

Following my father's death, my mother moved east in the beginning of July 1956 to be closer to her parents. A pregnancy check-up left everyone concerned that the shock of my father's death would affect my health as a baby in the womb. They told my mother that my fetal heartbeat had stopped. Upon hearing the doctor's words, my mother snapped out of the shock she was in and went on a long walk through the streets of Annapolis. She told me that she prayed, "Lord, if you save my son, I will give him back to you."

I was born later that day on July 11, 1956, a healthy eight pounds, 11 ounces.

Losing my dad but gaining a father

There is a truth in scripture that speaks to what every life is about. When God looked down from heaven, He looked for a champion to change the world. He chose a young man to make a difference. His name was Jeremiah. He wrote these words that God spoke over his life:

"Before I formed you in the womb I knew you, and before you were born I consecrated you; I have appointed you a prophet to the nations." Then I said, "Alas, Lord God! Behold, I do not know how to speak, because I am a youth." But the Lord said to me, "Do not say, 'I am a youth,' because everywhere I send you, you shall go, And all that I command you, you shall speak."

— *Jeremiah 1:5-7*

In a moment, a young boy was changed into a man through the words of a Father. Jeremiah went on to live a life that was anchored in those words. What struck me about this passage is that our calling predates our birth. In other words, you have always been on the mind of your Father in heaven. He has a plan and purpose for every life He creates. There has never been a moment when you have not been on His mind. There is a power and a freedom in living out of His love toward you.

Not long after I was born, my mother met another Navy officer named Dan McGlasson. They fell in love and got married. It was Dan who helped set the direction of my life by building structures that enabled me to effectively chase after my dreams. My stepfather was a motivator. He wanted me to excel. From cleaning my room to playing sports, he pushed me to be the best I could be.

Early one morning, he woke me up with an air horn, asking me one question, "Son, what do you want to be when you grow up?" At 5 o'clock in the morning, all I could see was a poster of Bob Hayes, the fastest man in the National Football League. I looked at him and said, "I want to become a professional football player." He said, "Great! It is now time to build a ladder to your dreams — one rung at a time."

Before I knew it, he had strapped a five-pound ankle

weight on each of my skinny 11-year-old legs and put new sneakers on my feet as we jumped into the car. He dropped me four miles from the house and said, "If you are going to do this, son, you have to outwork every other kid in America who is sleeping in right now. I am going to help you do this. I am going home to cook your breakfast. What do you want?" I remember ordering steak and eggs, blueberry pancakes, and orange juice. Then he just drove away!

I ran home that day with those five-pound ankle weights slipping up and down my skinny legs. And when I got home, breakfast was ready. There is nothing like eating a great meal after a good workout. (They don't call me Big Ed for nothing!) For years, I thought the reason hair didn't grow on my lower legs was because of the chafing of those five-pound Sears ankle weights.

My stepfather dropped me off five days a week throughout my high school years. That early morning structure in my life gave me a mental advantage over other athletes. I knew that I was gaining a day on every other high school athlete who was not getting up early. And it was because of my stepfather's willingness to help me reach my dreams that I eventually achieved them. I knew what he thought I was capable of.

My rite of passage

In the early 1970s, my stepfather commanded a diesel submarine called the *Tiranti Fish*. His duty with the Navy often led him away for months at a time. As a Navy family, we understood that the term "Med" meant the Mediterranean Sea, and that dad was leaving for at least three months to serve our country in the waters off the coast of Europe.

One day as his submarine was getting ready to depart for maneuvers in the Mediterranean Sea, my mother and I went down to the dock to say good-bye to him. With ceremonial colored smoke blasting out of the engines, the 300-foot *Tiranti Fish* started backing out of its berth. Then, my stepfather realized he had made two grave mistakes: He had driven the Volkswagen Beetle to the dock, and he still had the keys in his pocket!

My stepfather grabbed the bullhorn and shouted over the crowd of well-wishers, "Son, today you are a man. Drive your mother home." With that, he launched the keys through the air toward the dock and his 14-year-old stepson — and I snagged them before they hit the ground. I remember to this day the feeling of catching those keys with my left hand. Something happened to me that day when my stepfather declared over the whole crowd that I was a man. I remember grabbing the keys and looking at my mother and saying, "Let's go home."

There was just one problem — I had never driven.

My stepfather's mistake of not handing over the keys was an obvious one; driving the Volkswagen was not a readily apparent mistake. However, my mother's inexperience at driving a stick shift quickly revealed how much of a mistake it was. But there was no need to worry — I had just been declared a man, and learning to drive a stick shift was going to be easy, or so I thought.

After we got into the car, I turned the key in the ignition, not realizing that the car was in gear, or how to use the clutch. The car lurched forward a few feet through a shrub brush before coming to a sudden stop. My mother quickly began explaining her limited knowledge of clutch usage.

My next challenge was to find "reverse" on the stick. However, my stepfather had upgraded the stick shift knob to one with a walnut finish, only to affix it with the gears listed sideways. I cranked the ignition without stepping on the clutch again and launched the car through the bushes in front of us. Finally, I found reverse. But as I started backing out, I didn't quite trust the accelerator or the clutch. As I kept toggling those two pedals, it made an unpleasant jerking motion. While I kept trying to find first gear, I pressed the accelerator and rode the clutch. I was

bucking the car — and my mother — back and forth all
the way home for two miles with her screaming, "Would
you please stop doing that?!" But I made it home because
I was a man and my stepfather had said so. I don't think
my mother recovered for months from the whiplash I
gave her that day!

I knew something had changed in my 14-year-old
heart because of his pronouncement over me. It was an
accident, but his public declaration over me changed the
way I viewed myself. After that, it was hard for my
mother to get me to submit. We had many fights because
I misunderstood that being "the king" meant to serve her,
not to rule her. (But that's another story for another day.)

Developmental "handoffs"

In my quest to help my children identify milestones
in their lives, I started to look for some models in our culture. I discovered that in the Jewish tradition there are
three stages in the life of the child. First, there is a child's
relationship with his or her mother. It is the mom's
responsibility to handle the child's care until the child is
weaned. Next, the child is then given over to the dad until
he or she reaches the age of puberty — 12 for girls and
13 for boys. At that point, the child celebrates his or her
passage into adulthood: bar mitzvahs for boys and bat

mitzvahs for girls. (*Bar* means "son," and *mitzvah* means "of the law." You become a "son of the law.")

Through this ceremony, there is a definite handoff from the father to God, where a boy becomes a man. After the bar mitzvah, they are treated like men. Their mothers must release them into their new life. They are given more responsibility, including times of teaching and reading scripture.

They have now graduated.

> *"When I was a child, I acted like a child, but when I became a man, I put away childish things."*
> — *I Corinthians 13:11*

So many men are missing that kind of experience. Your father may have never proclaimed to the world that you are a man. He may have never passed down to you what it means to be a man — and how you transition into manhood where you follow your heart and chase your destiny. When your manhood is not in doubt, when you know who you are, you have all the confidence in the world to pursue your dreams.

In the following pages, I will share some tools that will help us become fathers who can make a difference in the lives of our kids. I want to answer the question many of us are asking: *What does my dad really think about me?* and *Have I arrived yet?* The answers to those questions will help us define our true identity and become all that God has made us capable of becoming. We will also talk about how to define a goal line for our kids, which will allow them to know and understand when they have "scored" in life.

There is a deep wound in many of us because we have never known the love of our fathers. But it doesn't have to remain a deep wound. God, our loving heavenly Father, can heal those wounds by helping us understand and accept His love for us. His love will call you out and declare over your life that you are a man in His eyes.

Now, there is a tremendous challenge for us as dads to pass that same experience along to our kids. We can create moments that let our kids know they have arrived — when we as dads throw up our hands in honor and say, "Touchdown! You're here." There is a similar moment when we become true sons to our heavenly Father — when we never again have to prove that we are sons, because the righteousness of Christ is deposited into our lives. We stop living for less and live for the joy He has set before us.

For Chapter One study guide and questions, visit: www.thedifferenceafathermakes.com

CHAPTER TWO

Living for Less
No More

In the movie *Seabiscuit*, we watch the transformation of a training horse to a champion thoroughbred. Despite Seabiscuit's ability to gallop at a fast pace, he was trained to lose. On the training grounds, Seabiscuit was not allowed to do what he was capable of doing — to run faster than all the other horses.

As Seabiscuit's transformation begins, there is an interesting conversation between owner Charles Howard and Tom Smith, Seabiscuit's trainer. With unsure legs, Seabiscuit is shown moving from side to side all around the track, unable to run in a straight line as if he is forever allowing the horses behind him to pass. Then Smith tells Howard, "He's so beat up, it's hard to tell what he's like. I can't help feeling they got him so screwed up running in a circle that he's forgotten what he was born to do. He just needs to learn how to be a horse again."

All those years of being held back from racing toward the finish beat down Seabiscuit. Then one glorious afternoon, he is turned loose in a pasture and rediscovers his identity — and, in the process, finds his purpose again. Seabiscuit eventually goes on to demonstrate his incredible ability to the world. While tending to an injured thoroughbred, Smith told Howard, "Every horse is good for something — you don't just throw a whole life away because he's banged up a little."

While watching that movie, my heart broke for all of those young people who have never had someone believe in them and throw them the keys. I meet them everyday, from bookstores to malls to coffee shops; yearning for a voice to call them out of their boredom, deeply wanting to make a difference, but forever coming in second. All Seabiscuit needed was a trainer who could see past his second place finishes and see he had the heart of a champion all along.

Seabiscuit's real life story ignited our country with hope that the little guy can make a difference in a time when we needed hope. The words of Seabiscuit's owner, Charles Howard, rang true, "Sometimes all a man needs is a second chance."

How does God fix a broken human race horse?

He strips away our self-imposed limitations and reminds us who we really are, exposing the lies that have kept us believing that coming in second is the best we can do. As Christ enters into our life, He brings His kingdom; transformation begins in our heart. A new way of living begins to shape us as His love and Word rebuild our minds with the truth that we are the objects of His Father's love, and He has made us to make a difference in the world.

Do you feel yourself living for second? Here is a story from the Bible that helped me in my journey.

Settling for the east side of the Jordan

There is a distinct difference between a man who is focused on simply surviving and a man who is committed to thriving. The thriver is exacting every ounce of juice from life that is possible. He lives life to the fullest; he goes for the gusto. The survivor simply exists, looking to make it through the day.

In the book of Numbers, we find all of Israel on the cusp of crossing the Jordan River and about to press into the Promised Land after wandering in the desert for 40 years. But God gave Joshua permission to take His people into the Promised Land, the land that they had dreamed about.

The day arrived to cross over the river, but some of the Israelites, namely the children of Reuben, were simply looking for safety, not abundance. They were afraid of the challenges that crossing over into the Promised Land might entail. They were willing to settle for less than God had in store for them. They told Moses, "If we have found favor in your sight, let this land be given to your servants as a possession; *do not take us across the Jordan*" (Numbers 32:5, *emphasis mine*).

After 40 years of living on the edge of seizing the bounty God has promised them, they were captured by a fear that they would not make it and the "giants" on the other side of the river would defeat them.

What do you do when confronted with change and an uncertain future? They acted like businessmen, weighing the risks and benefits. They decided it would be better to remain on the east side of the Jordan River. Moses promptly chastised them: "Shall your brothers go to war while you yourselves sit here? Now why are you discouraging the sons of Israel from crossing over into the land which the Lord has given them? This is what your fathers did when I sent them from Kadesh Barnea to see the land" (Numbers 32:6-8).

Ultimately, the children of Reuben chose to fight in the battle. But they risked their lives to fight for something they didn't think they could have. After all of the battles were through, they unbelievably settled for less and returned to the east side of the river. Unwilling to take the inheritance that was due them on the west side of the Jordan, they crossed back over the river.

In the midst of the river, one of Reuben's sons realized that their tribe and children were now going to be separated from the rest of the tribes of Israel by this river. They decided to build a monument next to the river to remind their people and kids that they were part of the great things God had done. Reuben's sons were saying, "I want my sons and my sons' children to know that dad used to be somebody." Ouch!

Was that attempt at misdirection, at covering their tracks, successful? The saddest footnote to the story of Reuben is what Deborah sings about them in the book of Judges:

"In the districts of Reuben there was much searching of heart. Why did you stay among the campfires to hear the whistling for the flocks?"

— *Judges 5:15-16, NIV*

I have learned that when you settle for less than what God designed you for, you'll settle for monuments and trophies over the movements and future adventures of God.

Are you settling for safety and a nice flock of sheep? Will you choose to build a monument to your compromises, rather than build a bold and fruitful life? What kind of man will you be? What will you instill in your children — courage or fear? Will you stay east of God's promises, instead of living in the land where you trust God to defeat your giants?

> When you settle for less than what God designed you for, you'll settle for monuments and trophies over the movements and future adventures of God.

What happened to the children of Reuben that caused them to settle for less? It is found in the story of their father. For Reuben, being the oldest son meant that the blessing of his father Jacob would one day be his. A father's blessing was the most powerful thing that was given from father to son. That blessing was so sought after that Reuben's father, Jacob, tricked his own father for it. Reuben watched his father give his blessing to his youngest brother, Joseph. With no blessing received, Reuben had nothing to give his children. So, they learned to settle for less.

Fatherlessness

In order to experience the fullness of life that God has for us, we must first connect to our heavenly Father. One of the reasons we have so much difficulty in connecting to the heart of the Father — and even our earthly fathers — is because sin severed that relationship. Before sin entered the world, Adam and Eve lived in the fullness of what God intended. There was no pain, no suffering, no death. Adam and Eve had dominion over everything. Then the enemy began to worm his way into the picture.

When Adam and Eve chose to eat the forbidden fruit, they chose to "father" their own lives. They didn't realize they were about to experience spiritual death by breaking their close relationship with their heavenly Father. In the moment sin entered the world, creation became fatherless.

For many years, the common man's only approach to God was through the blood of bulls, goats, and lambs. God set up a way for man to experience redemption from sin, but it wasn't a relationship. They wouldn't even pronounce God's name. For most of the writers in the Old Testament, God as their Father was a distant concept.

But God did not give up on mankind. He made a way to restore that relationship and bring back the heart of the Father to us. When Jesus came onto the scene, He came not only to pay the price for sin and separation from God, but He came out of the tomb and rose again to give us a relationship with His Father. Philip said, "Show us the Father — that will be enough." Jesus said, "If you have seen Me, you have seen the Father." The disciples must have thought, "So, that's what the Father looks like: kind, compassionate, loving, affirming. He came to love us, heal us, and accept us for who we are." That must have turned their preconceptions upside down! They came to realize God wasn't an angry being on a distant mountain. They began to understand that the Father wanted to come down and have relationship with them.

You see, it's the life of the Father who makes the ultimate difference in life. It's the life of my heavenly Father who ultimately made the difference in my life, and who wants to make a difference right now in your life.

Real fathering

I have learned that it takes a father to call out the magnificent destiny in his children. Boys can't call out men, girls can't call out women. It takes a father. And it doesn't simply take any father — it takes a father who is in rich relationship with his kids.

CBS aired a special called "The Greatest Moments in Olympic History." They included the British runner

Derek Redman as he prepared for the 1988 Olympic Games in Seoul, South Korea. He suffered a terrible injury that led to 22 surgeries. After training his whole life for the Olympics, he wasn't about to let an injury prevent him from pursuing his dream. To the shock of many track and field pundits, Redman qualified for the 400-meter race for the 1992 Olympic Games in Barcelona, Spain. Just to be competing in the Olympics was an amazing feat. But as the starting gun was fired, Redman had no idea he was about to endure another twist of cruel fate.

Halfway around the track, Redman was in the middle of the pack when he pulled a hamstring and tumbled to the ground. Stunned and grieving, Redman was determined to finish the race. He staggered to his feet and began limping around the track, tearful, embarrassed, and grimacing in obvious pain. Indeed, the pain appeared too much for Redman to bear alone, and it looked as if he would collapse on the track.

Suddenly, a man came racing from the stands across the track to Redman's side. He put his hand onto Redman's shoulder, just as he collapsed into the man's arms. The man began to assist Redman in making it across the finish line. To the amazement and delight of the spectators, the twosome hobbled forward together — slowly, achingly, step-by-step — for the remainder of the race. As they finally crossed the finish line together, the crowd rose to its feet, applauding and cheering the portrait of courage, determination, and shared commitment they had just witnessed.

Following the race, everyone learned that the man who helped Redman was none other than his father, Jim Redman. After years of waking up at 4 o'clock in the morning to facilitate his son's pursuit of his dream, the elder Redman had one thing to say to his son on that track, "Derek, we started this thing together, and we are going to finish this thing together."

Is that the kind of father who raised you? Would your dad have rushed to your side to help you fulfill your dream if you were in Derek Redman's position?

Let me ask you another question: How do you feel your heavenly Father responds when you fall or fail? Do you envision a God who would be even quicker to your side than Derek's dad? Or has your assumption been that God would be ashamed of your failed effort, disgusted because you had not been sufficiently prepared, or embarrassed because you had not won the race?

Do you long to hear your earthly father say, "You're the son I always wanted," or "You make me proud, son" — but he's either not around or incapable of doing so? Are you ready for God to heal that wound, and to declare your identity as a man?

Jesus came not only to heal us from our sin, but to introduce us to a Father whose attitude toward us is one of joy so great that He sings and rejoices over us. Did you know there is a musical celebration emanating from the Father's heart over your life everyday? But to hear it, you have to receive what Christ did for you. Maybe you have never given your life to Christ, or you don't know how. I will share a prayer with you that I prayed in 1977 when I gave my life to Christ:

> **Did you know there is a musical celebration emanating from the Father's heart over your life everyday?**

"Dear Jesus, I realize that my sin has separated me from Your love. I ask You to forgive me, and I receive what You gave me on the Cross — the forgiveness of my sin. And I receive the new life that You gave us when You came out of the tomb. I confess that You are the only way that I can be forgiven and be saved from my sins. In Jesus' name, amen."

If you just prayed that prayer for the first time, I've got great news for you: Your name has been written in heaven. That's how a man is born again. I encourage you to share with a trusted friend about the prayer you just prayed. Find someone you know who loves Jesus and ask them to help you begin your journey. (If we can serve you, contact us at our website: www.thedifferenceafathermakes.com)

A father's calling

Understanding what it means to be a father to your children is a process, one that takes time and a determination to make fathering one of your highest priorities.

Not long after I married a beautiful Southern California blonde, my lovely wife Jill and I started having kids. I remember the moment my first son Edward was born. I held up little Edward and realized I was now a dad. In one sense, it was the proudest day of my life; but on the other hand, I was terrified. I didn't know what to do or how to be a dad. How do I raise this kid? How do I help him transition from being a boy to being a man? How do I help him discover the song that God has locked in his heart?

In Ephesians 1:18-19, Paul explains that there is something God has placed inside each of us — and He wants to bring it to light: "I pray that the eyes of your heart may be enlightened, so that you will know what is the hope of His calling, what are the riches of the glory of His inheritance in the saints, and what is the surpassing greatness of His power toward us who believe."

For every person, there is a secret in God's heart about who he or she is meant to be. It is our job as fathers to help our children discover their own story and secret, and to declare that over their lives. Once I became a father, I set myself to look at scripture to find out how to unlock this calling.

For Chapter Two study guide and questions,
visit: www.thedifferenceafathermakes.com

CHAPTER THREE

Developing Rites
of Passage

Early in our marriage, my wife and I committed to making lasting memories with our kids. While I am tirelessly bent on changing the world every day and afraid to miss a minute of the action, she makes sure we get our rest, namely in the form of family vacations. One summer we packed both our cars — one with all our fun vacation necessities, and the other with our five kids and Labrador retriever — and headed up to Mammoth Mountain.

After we arrived and began unpacking the car, my wife approached me and told me our 11-year-old son, Edward, was upset. I was curious why anyone would be upset at the beginning of our family vacation.

"Why is Edward upset?" I asked my wife.

"He said that every year when we come up to

Mammoth Mountain he never gets to do what he wants to do," my wife said.

"What are you talking about?" I asked, befuddled. "We go fishing. We go hiking."

"Yeah, but he doesn't feel like you want to do what he wants to do," my wife explained.

"Well, what does he want to do?" I asked.

"You need to ask him," my wife said.

So, I wandered over toward Edward and began to find out what he really wanted to do.

I said, "Hey, Edward, what do you want to do on vacation?"

"Really?" Edward asked with uncertainty.

"Yeah," I said. "Don't you want to go fly fishing? Remember that big fish you caught last year in your float tube?"

"No, dad, I don't like fly fishing," Edward answered.

"Why?" I asked.

"Well, I keep hanging up my fly rod in the trees and then you yell at me," Edward said. "I break off all my leaders, and I keep slipping and falling in the stream and start floating downstream — you yell at me for spooking the fish. It's just no fun, dad!"

In that moment, the Lord showed me how focused I was on myself. Even on our family vacations, my goal had been to do what I wanted to do. Suddenly, there was a real change occurring in my heart toward my kids. I was doing what every other dad does. I was making a living, building a life for them, having fun with them. But when I looked deep inside, I realized that the vacations were all about me and what I wanted to do for rest. That's when I realized God wanted to do something big in my life: Turn my heart toward my kids.

Let them choose?

I then asked Edward, "What do you want to do then?"

He said, "I want to go mountain biking on the top of Mammoth Mountain. Let's take the gondola to the top and ride down."

Now I had done it. We packed up the car with the necessary first aid equipment, helmets, aspirin and drove to the lodge at Mammoth Mountain.

I remember thinking, "What in the world are you thinking?" as we were loading our bikes into the bike rack on the gondola. Of course, I acted cool on the outside, but inside I was terrified. I kept thinking of the Wide World of Sports advertisement of "the thrill of victory and the agony of defeat." I couldn't even look out the window as my son chided me to look at how high we were.

We arrived at the top with the winds blowing over 30 miles per hour. Edward said, "Follow me, dad." This was my first mistake. He chose to go down the Kamikaze run first. The name was indicative of the steepness of the descent and the craziness of the rider. I had totally forgotten about the safety of my son as I had to apply maximum brake pressure to slow down my muscular 325-pound frame as we sped down the Kamikaze. Even with full brake pressure, the slowest I could go was 35 miles an hour. The other hazard that day was the switchback turns where soft areas of decomposed granite had been built up. The idea for maneuvering these turns is to sit back on your bike so your front wheel doesn't dig in.

Three different times my front wheel dug into the soft slope, launching me end over end. I think I did a triple flip once!

My son looked down at me, sprawled out on my back with my toe clips still attached, and said, "Are you okay, dad? I've never seen anyone do that before." I was so grateful for the mercy of God that I survived and didn't breaking anything.

Maybe you're there today, and your vacations are about polishing your Harley, fulfilling your desires, doing what only you want to do. This might be a good time to lean down to your son and say, "Hey, son, what do you

want to do?" Just a word of advice: Stay away from the
Kamikaze run.

Young Jesus in the temple

As God began to turn my heart toward my children,
I began to search the scriptures for ways that I could be a
better father and assist my kids as they transitioned into
adulthood. What I found was some interesting insight into
young Jesus' own rite of passage.

> *And when they saw Him, they were astonished; and His
> mother said to Him, "Son, why have You treated us this way?
> Behold, Your father and I have been anxiously looking for You."
> And [Jesus] said to them, "Why is it that you were looking for Me?
> Did you not know that I had to be in My Father's house?"*
> — Luke 2:48-49

For years, this passage of scripture puzzled me.
Jesus had been separated from His parents for three days.
Can you imagine the emotional state of a mother who had
lost her son for three days? Now imagine if you had lost
the Messiah? Can you picture how frantically Mary
searched through every place she had been? She was
probably screaming just like every other mother who cannot immediately locate her child. She wanted to know how

Jesus could have done this to His mother. But Jesus asked her, "Why is it you were looking for me?"

What a curious question from Jesus! The reason they were looking for Him was because they left Him. This was Jesus' version of the movie *Home Alone*. He had slipped away from the family caravan and found his way to the temple. Jesus responded to his mother's query by saying, "Did you not know that I had to be in My Father's house?" The King James Version of the Bible says of Mary and Joseph, "They reckoned it not." In other words, Mary was scratching her head over Jesus' answer. She had no idea what Jesus meant by His response.

One day over lunch, a Jewish friend of mine, Rabbi Steven Berkowitz, clarified the cultural context of this passage for me. The fact that Luke points out Jesus' age is significant. According to Jewish tradition, if a Jewish boy had no father, he went to the temple to answer questions in order to prove he was worthy to be bar mitzvahed at age 13. Jesus had no earthly father. That's when it hit me: Jesus was beginning His own rite of passage. He was engaging a tradition that would help move Him from boyhood to manhood.

How does God turn a boy who has no earthly father into a man and a father? Jesus was an orphan on earth. And yet He became a man through the love of His heavenly Father.

You might be coming from a place where your father may be dead — literally or spiritually. You may not have had the experience of his voice speaking your identity into you. Is it too late? Is it too late for you to do this for your kids? Is it too late to make a lasting difference?

We find that Jesus' journey is the same journey He came to model for us. Through God's power, the very foundation of our lives can be changed. It's never too late.

Making His Father proud

Another story about Jesus that struck me occurred on the day of His baptism — His grand commissioning day. Jesus was 30 years old when He went to the river where His cousin John was baptizing people and calling them to repentance.

Then Jesus arrived from Galilee at the Jordan coming to John, to be baptized by him. But John tried to prevent Him, saying, "I have need to be baptized by You, and do You come to me?" But Jesus answering said to him, "Permit it at this time; for in this way it is fitting for us to fulfill all righteousness." Then he permitted Him. After being baptized, Jesus came up immediately from the water; and behold, the heavens were opened, and he saw the Spirit of God descending as a dove and lighting on Him, and behold, a voice

*out of the heavens said, "This is My beloved Son, in whom I am
well-pleased."*

— *Matthew 3:13-17*

After Jesus' baptism, the heavens opened and a
voice said, "This is My beloved Son, in whom I am well-
pleased." Why the voice from heaven? That struck me as
peculiar. God obviously was very proud of Jesus. But was
there more to the story?

For a while, I thought it was done for John the
Baptist's sake, but then I realized that John already knew
who Jesus was. Could it have been that, in that moment,
God was modeling before the whole world the principle
that every man and woman needs to clearly hear how God
feels about them? God loves every man, woman, boy, and
girl with the deepest love. And we need to hear it, not
only from our earthly fathers, but also from our heavenly
Father.

As I learned more about Jewish culture, I realized an
even greater significance related to God's pronouncement
over Jesus at the Jordan River. During a bar mitzvah, in
the moment when a father holds his son up to God, he
proclaims over him in Hebrew, "This is my beloved Son in
whom I am well pleased!" This was what happened with
Jesus: Our Father in heaven hoisted Jesus onto His shoul-

ders before the entire world and told everyone how pleased He was with Jesus' life.

You are my beloved son! You are my beloved daughter! That is the goal line sons and daughters want to cross with their dads before they enter into adulthood. You don't want to wonder what your father thinks about you — you want to know it, and know it with confidence. Those questions that might haunt them in the night — "Does dad really love me?" or "What does dad think of me?" — are erased with a resounding proclamation of love by their father.

> You don't want to wonder what your father thinks about you — you want to know it, and know it with confidence.

Armed with this insight, I started to think about what I could do for my oldest son, Edward.

Edward's rite of passage

The principles I found in Jesus' story were two-fold: the public declaration of the love of the Father, and the articulation of a goal line. Those principles made me want to create a moment that would make a significant difference in the lives of my children — a moment after which there would no longer be a question in my kids' minds or hearts about what I think about them.

After hearing a friend of mine share about rites of passage and the transition of his own sons into manhood, I began to formulate a plan for how I would transition my kids into adulthood. When Edward turned 13 years old, I put my plan into action.

One Sunday morning in front of our entire church, I called Edward forward. As he was joining me up front, I said, "I've never done this before, but I feel like the Lord wants me to publicly acknowledge and affirm my son." Before the congregation, I began to affirm all the things in my son that I loved about him. I knew well that this could be the moment that could change his life because I knew it was changing me as I spoke those words over him. As I was praying for him and speaking into his life, I said, "I believe in you. And from this day, son, you are no longer a boy. You are a man."

In that moment, the congregation leaped to its feet and celebrated as my son and I embraced. I had answered the question in his mind, and perhaps in the minds of those in our community — and now it was time to dance in the end zone.

That day was significant in the life of my son Edward. Not long afterward during a Promise Keeper's event, my son had an experience with the Father and received fresh direction for his life.

Obviously, you might not have the opportunity to place your son or daughter in front of a crowd or a church. But you can do something just as dramatic. It is not the size of the crowd that your kids want; it is just your sold out heart for them.

My next challenge was to figure out how to call out my oldest daughter, Jessica.

Jessica's rite of passage

To us guys, girls are very hard to understand, whether they are six years old or 60 years old. However, thankfully, they are not impossible! While the charge of calling out a daughter may seem more difficult than calling out a son, it can be done in a way that wins your daughter's heart forever.

So, how do you call out a little girl? What does she want? What does she need?

Putting together a rite of passage for Jessica took more time than I thought it would. I started praying about what to do, while trying to figure her out. How many of you guys are still trying to figure out your wives or daughters? It may take you another hundred years! It's true — they are beautifully created, but sometimes hard to understand.

So, I finally devised a plan. I took my daughter to an Italian restaurant and bought her a promise ring with little diamonds embedded in the band, and I hid the ring inside a flower. This outing wasn't completely awkward because, long before this night, my daughters and I had gotten into a practice of dating. The Lord showed me that if I dated my daughters, I wouldn't lose their hearts when they got older. I believe my daughters' ability to hold off boys' physical passes is directly related to the love and affection I sowed into their lives. Sometimes, my daughters fight over whose turn it is to go on a date with dad.

During my dinner with Jessica, I spent the first portion of our time telling her all the things I liked about her. As I talked, her eyes were welling up with tears. Mine were also. Nervous and excited, I felt somewhat like I did when I asked Jill to marry me. Deep down, I knew this moment would change Jessica's life.

As I was deciding how I wanted to help my daughters cross this child-to-adult goal line, I decided to model the experience of how a man would propose marriage to them. I bent down low, leaned in close toward her and said, "Jessica, I am giving you this ring today. Are you willing to make a covenant before the Lord tonight, that on your wedding night you will be prepared to present this ring to your husband and say to him, 'This ring represents a covenant I made with my dad, that I would save myself until I got married. And I have done so'? Will you wear this ring?"

Jessica just started weeping. And as I slipped the ring on her finger and said, "Jessica, I'm here to tell you that from this moment on, you are no longer a little girl — you are a woman." I also began to cry.

She remained very emotional as I began to tell her the things I would promise to do to protect, to lead, and to guide her. The people in the restaurant who were close by were weeping with us. Some people who were sitting far away assumed I was proposing, and were saying, "How sick! Look at that old guy proposing to that young girl!" But I must say, we do live in California and so there were also a few guys saying, "Cool, dude! Go for it." Slowly, the news began to trickle through the restaurant that it was a dad who had just declared his daughter to be a woman.

As I reflect on the life of my daughter since that moment, the growth in Jessica's life has been remarkable. The responsibility she has taken on, the person she has become — she is truly a woman. Why? Because her Father in heaven spoke through her father on earth and declared it so. That's crossing the goal line.

That's the beginning.

Life after crossing the goal line?

If your heart is stirred to go out and declare your sons to be men and your daughters to be women, remember: This is merely a mile marker in the exciting journey you get to take with your children. Some steps may involve rites of passage, but there are many more steps to take together. I wish I could say that all you need to do is have a dinner with your daughter and call her out into womanhood. I'm sure you know by now that parenting is much more than that. It's about building structure in your children's lives and helping to order what happens. It's about helping your sons and daughters transition into adulthood.

While your son might be a man in your eyes, it may take time for your wife to release her son. Both of you will need to learn to stop giving advice when your kids don't ask for it. Shift to using mentoring and coaching skills; ask questions to help them process their decisions. For me, it took a mental shift from seeing my son as "my boy," whom I could command and control, to transitioning to the next phase of our relationship in which I now treat him more like one of my friends.

To help my son navigate into adulthood, I now ask him what he thinks he needs to do instead of giving suggestions. And I learned I had to do it in such a way that he really knew I trusted his judgment. Then one day, the Lord showed me a way to melt my son's heart. He showed me that I need to become vulnerable before my son and let him love me by saying, "Son, I'm having a problem here. I need your advice."

I remember a specific moment like that with Edward. When I asked for his advice, he said, "Really? You're the pastor, dad!" Then he shared with me what he would do. I remember his chest sticking out a little farther and watching his confidence grow. He knew what his father thought about him. I didn't just ask him because I wanted to patronize him — I really needed some advice. And the Lord used him to speak to me.

Just as in the Jewish tradition, you are passing your children to the Lord, equipping them to hear the voice of their Father in heaven by helping them hear the love and commitment in your own voice. You want to help them hear and feel God's call on their lives. The success in your children's lives is not simply determined by your rites of passage with them; rather, it's directly related to how well you connect them to the voice of their heavenly Father who can lead them into their destiny.

There is no magic formula for making a great kid! However, raising children who are passionate about God and about their own futures is dependent upon your ability to equip them to live a life that honors both themselves and God. Rites of passage are simply practices that can help them live like Jesus lived.

But how did Jesus, who experienced a rite of passage with His heavenly Father, live?

I have some missionary friends who have been serving in Mozambique for over seven years amidst some of the poorest people on the planet. Despite rampant poverty, God has poured out His Spirit in that country and revival is occurring. Over 5,000 new churches have been planted during this move of God. Recently, they sent me a note about their travels and what it's like to be living among such poverty. The last line of their note struck me: "We're here living in the smile of our Father."

I realized that was exactly how Jesus lived — under the smile of his Father. How did he do that?

For Chapter Three study guide and questions, visit: www.thedifferenceafathermakes.com

CHAPTER FOUR

Living in the Smile
of the Father

There comes a time in every man's life when he stops and evaluates his life. He asks himself, "Am I a success? Am I becoming all I am supposed to become? Is my life honoring God?"

After serving as a pastor for 20 years, I recently came to that point in my own life. It's easy to look at the past and feel like you've blown it and are far from where you *should* be. At 47 years old, I felt like I had experienced some great successes with my kids. On the other hand, there were some parts of my life that I felt weren't measuring up. So I went before the Lord and asked the question, "Father, how am I doing?"

As I was sitting on a restaurant patio overlooking the harbor in Newport Beach, I desperately longed to hear God speak words of encouragement into my life. I was weary from the journey and thirsty for refreshment in my soul. Just as that feeling began to settle over me, I began reading in Judges 15 about Samson. Like me, Samson was weary from the journey.

> *Then [Samson] became very thirsty, and he called to the Lord and said, "You have given this great deliverance by the hand of your servant, and now shall I die of thirst and fall into the hands of the uncircumcised?*
> — *Judges 15:18*

That's where I was — broken, tired, and weary from dealing with challenges in my ministry. I was crying out to God for connection, validation, and refreshment.

> *But God split the hollow place that is in Lehi so that water came out of it. When he drank, his strength returned and he revived. Therefore he named it En-hakkore, which is in Lehi to this day.*
> — *Judges 15:19*

God heard Samson.
God heard me.
As I was reading these words, I noticed, out of the corner of my eye, a previously dormant fountain in the restaurant had just been turned on, and was now bubbling over! Then the worship music I was listening to through

my headphones began piping in the lyrics of a song by Michael W. Smith that said, "I can hear Your voice." And the Lord began to speak to me.

While I was praying and listening to the Lord, I recorded these words in my journal: "I just want to please You, Father. You became my Father after You took mine. I never had his voice, but I have Yours. I don't want to miss You right now." The next moment, God's words flooded my heart. He said to me, "You can't, Ed. You are a man after My heart." The Lord then went on to describe all of the sacrifices He has witnessed in my life. God was not scowling about my life — He was smiling!

We need to be men who live for the smile of our Father, not for the trophies of this world. In that moment with the Lord, all that mattered, and all that still matters, is that I'm His son. The words He spoke to me filled me like that spring filled the thirsty Samson who had just slain a thousand Philistines. I began sobbing softly in the restaurant. Patrons slowly moved away from my table. And God's love began to wash over me as it became real to me that His smile is over my life.

What we really want

Have you ever had a moment in your time with the Lord when He asks you the question, "What do you want?" and you know He is going to give it to you? Deep down, you know you better ask for something meaningful. During that moment with the Lord, I had before me a number of potential directions and adventures to choose from. But I remember saying, "I just want to be Your son." And I simply broke.

You see, the moment you know what's really important in your life, it changes you. You realize it's not how much you do but who you are. How quickly we slip into works and move from the grace that is freely given to us, to trying to prove that we are worthy of His grace. It's a slippery slope in life, isn't it?

In the end, you want the same thing your children want most — to be the child of a father who smiles upon your life as you chase your dreams. Once we understand how to live for the smile of the Father, we can be fathers who smile on our children. Once we understand that we no longer have to earn His approval, we can bask in the freedom of living for His smile. Just like a little child, we can walk and play in the field of our dreams, and turn around to see if our Father is smiling. And He is.

Experiencing God's smile

Growing up, my whole life was about becoming a football player. As I shared earlier, my stepfather helped build some boundaries and practices into my life that enabled me to reach my dreams. Each day as he dropped me off four miles from our house and drove home to make me breakfast, he challenged me to be the best I could be — to become the man I was made to be. He called me out to be a man. But nothing he did could prepare me for the devastating blow to my dreams that occurred on a practice field in Youngstown, Ohio.

During a routine practice, an eager freshman dove for a loose ball, diving right into my left knee. As soon as he made impact with me, I heard and felt my knee rip. The trainers rushed me to the hospital where the doctors told me I had torn all three major ligaments in my knee and would require reconstructive surgery the next morning. I was shocked. In a single moment, my hope was stolen. *Would I ever play football again?* I wondered. They put a soft cast on my knee, gave me a number of ice bags, and sent me back to the dormitory.

Alone and scared, I sat in Kilcawley Hall at Youngstown State, wondering about my future, when a campus minister knocked on my door. It was Bill. I had met him earlier on campus. He asked if he could come in and talk to me because he had heard about my injury. Bill asked, "Can I share a verse of scripture with you, Ed?" So he did and then added, "Ed, you've got a lot of things going for you, but you lack one thing — and that's a personal relationship with Jesus." I remember looking at him and saying, "What can Jesus do for me here?" He shared the Gospel story with me and read a single verse I had never heard before: "For God so loved the world, that He gave His only begotten Son, that whoever believes in Him shall not perish, but have eternal life."

I didn't understand why God would do that for me; but I knew I was in trouble, and I was broken. I also knew for the first time that I had tried to pay for all of my own sin — and I couldn't do it anymore. So I received Christ that day. I asked Him to come into my heart and pay for my sin. After I prayed, Bill did something he said later was out of character for him to do. He reached out and laid his hand on my ice bag and prayed a simple prayer, "Jesus, heal Ed's knee."

I didn't feel anything. My knee was still swollen and numb. But I had this assurance inside of me like I had never had before. I knew God loved me — He had sent someone to pray for me. However, I tossed and turned all night. It's difficult to sleep with ice bags around your legs!

The next morning, the trainer came to take me to the hospital. I couldn't feel much in my leg because of the cast. They led me into a waiting room and made me put on one of those robes that don't tie all the way around even a normal-sized man. After that, they rolled me down the hallway to do an arthogram; they shot colored dye into my knee to determine what kind of surgery I needed. In those days, they didn't have the scope technique. It was slice and dice.

After Dr. Michael Vuksta, our team physician, studied the X-rays, he began shaking his head. He looked at me and said, "Here are the X-rays of your knee yesterday, and here they are today. I don't understand it, but somehow all of your ligaments have been reattached. There is nothing wrong with your knee." Those words struck me, breaking me emotionally and spiritually.

> He found a broken football player in Youngstown, Ohio, and gave me a new beginning.

There's a Father who always loves us. He found a broken football player in Youngstown, Ohio, and gave me a new beginning.

I jumped off the gurney table to test my knee. It wasn't wobbly at all. I started jumping up and down and shouting "Hallelujah!" I had seen Richard Pryor do that in a movie, so I figured that's how you thank God!

After I left the hospital, I went on a long walk. I was crying. God had just healed me and touched me. I couldn't wait to tell someone what had happened. As I sat down on a bench, I remember praying and feeling the words of God come into my heart. I had been asking Him most of the day, "What do You want me to do with my life?" And I heard these words, "I want you to play pro football, but when I call for your life back, I want you to give it back to me." I said, "You want me to play pro football? If I knew You were this cool, I would've given my life to You a long time ago!"

I was fully expecting He would ask me to do something that was boring and uneventful. But God wanted me to play football! This was exciting news to me. However, the second part of the statement I didn't understand.

For the first time in my life, I was living in the smile of my heavenly Father. I knew He loved me — and I loved Him. It wasn't about what I did; it was about whose son I was.

How Jesus lived in His Father's smile

Have you ever wondered how Jesus lived each day under the smile of His Father? After calling the church to lay aside everything that keeps us from experiencing God's promises, the writer of Hebrews explains how we can run the race just like Jesus, living each moment in the complete acceptance of God's love and tenderness for us:

> *Therefore, since we have so great a cloud of witnesses sur-*
> *rounding us, let us also lay aside every encumbrance and the sin*
> *which so easily entangles us, and let us run with endurance the race*
> *that is set before us, fixing our eyes on Jesus, the author and perfecter*
> *of faith, who for the joy set before Him endured the cross, despising*
> *the shame, and has sat down at the right hand of the throne of*
> *God.*
>
> — *Hebrews 12:1-2*

Do you see it? "The joy set before Him." Jesus lived for the smile of His Father, for the good things He knew God had in store for Him. He was much less concerned about His current challenges and pain than He was about the vision the Father had given Him concerning His role in the Kingdom. In the Gospel of John, Jesus communicates the depth of relationship He has with God: *"I have made Your name known to them, and will make it known, so that the love wherewith You loved Me may be in them, and I in them"* (John 17:26).

Do you love your kids with the same intention with which God loves you, so that "the love wherewith He loves you may be in them"?

Christ came to give us a living relationship with both Him and His Father. He was so enamored with His love for the Father that He said, "I only do what I hear the Father saying and do what the Father is doing." To mankind who has the choice to walk away, Jesus constantly modeled what the Father does. Jesus then modeled how to live a life He ultimately had to give just so we could have the same relationship He had with the Father.

My youngest son, Joshua, lives the way I want to live. Recently, while we were throwing the baseball, he was scorching my hand with the speed of his pitches from 15 feet away. Every pitch was with all his strength.

I asked him, "Josh, could you throw it a little slower? You are breaking my hand." He simply replied, "I can't, dad. I just have a powerful arm."

He runs the same way, with all his heart. I admire the courage and release he lives in. I wonder if that is what Jesus was trying to teach His disciples when He told them that the Kingdom of God must be entered like a little child would enter. That courage only emerges from a deep trust.

As fathers, we must be diligent to instill in our children the difference between living under the smile of their Father versus feeling their need to earn His smile. We do this by modeling God's love for them — your love for them is not based on what they do, but is based simply on the fact that they are your son or daughter. And we teach them how God's love for them operates in the same manner. As they begin to understand this concept, they will naturally gravitate toward pursuing the dreams God has placed in their own hearts.

Smiles to dreams

After I finished playing at Youngstown State, I was off to the National Football League. I remember going to rookie camp in Hempstead, New York, in my brand new van with a custom paint job. I rolled my new TV, stereo, and refrigerator on a dolly into my dorm only to learn that rookies have to walk the stairs to the seventh floor. A veteran came up to me and said, "Hey, rookie, looks like you're planning to stay." To which I responded, "I didn't come to leave." I knew in my heart that I was supposed to be there.

On the training camp depth chart, I was listed as the seventh center. They had drafted heavily for centers that season — and I was last in line. Throughout training camp, I watched the favor of the Lord move me all the way to second on the depth chart. And my career went like professional athletic careers go. I played for the Jets, and then moved to play with the Los Angeles Rams. Then I came back to New York for a year to play with the Giants before I joined the Philadelphia Eagles.

One night during training camp with the Eagles, I

couldn't sleep. Have you ever had one of those nights when you just can't sleep because you know the Lord wants to speak to you about something? So I grabbed my Bible and went for a walk out on the field. As I was walking, I heard the Lord say, "Give it back and preach the Gospel."

I was reluctant to give it back. I was living what I thought was my dream. I had worked very hard to achieve it. I resisted that still small voice. On the first snap of practice the next morning I tore the ligaments in my knee again, effectively ending my career. It was the Lord's way of awakening me to my next dream — a dream that would end up being significantly more fulfilling than yesterday's tired dream, which I was trying so desperately to hang on to. With my understanding of God's unconditional love for me, I began to pursue with complete abandonment the new dream He placed in my heart. Since I knew He loved me no matter what, where was the risk? I couldn't disappoint Him by pursuing the dreams He instilled in me.

Do you ever wonder why your own dreams seem so far away, and you feel you just can't get there? Jesus modeled for us how to achieve our dreams as we live for the smile of the Father. I have come to realize there are three things that every dream requires: a price, a despising of shame, and an understanding of what God wants to give you.

The first thing that every dream requires is a price. "For the joy set before Him," Jesus endured the cross. Dreams aren't free; in fact, they can be quite costly. To take up your cross means you have to be willing to deny current pleasures and distractions for long-term gain. So many times, Christ came to that moment when He had to deny himself rather than grabbing His rights. Though He was God, He laid it down and became a bond servant and a slave. Every dream that is worthwhile has a price attached — a trade-off that requires you to say "no" to something else you value. But if you can live under the smile of your Father, the trade-offs don't matter. You don't care anymore about them.

Every dream requires despising shame. That's what Jesus had to endure when He carried the cross. He accepted the role his Father gave Him, even though in the world's eyes He should have felt foolish and ashamed. Can you imagine the Son of God being publicly disrobed and crucified in that fashion? I know many of you reading this book have seen the movie, *The Passion of the Christ*. What an amazing work of art! Some people say it is too brutal. Others say it was not even close to what Christ endured. Every Kingdom-based dream carries with it the risk that the world will not understand. Things that are heaven-sent and Kingdom-bound require a "foolish" level of faith and trust. How do you do that? How many times have you stepped out in faith, hoping that it was the Lord?

Every dream requires an understanding of what God wants to give you. Jesus "sat down at the right hand of the Father." To achieve everything God has called you to do, you have to be willing to sit in that seat, and the make all the trade-offs required. There is no way to do that unless you know you are loved, and know whose son you are. The one who names you determines your destiny. The one who names you determines how you will face the sacrifice, the shame, and the seat. If it's not out of the voice of the father, the seat will ultimately not be a good fit. Have you ever met someone who has built his whole life around someone else's approval, then realized he had leaned his ladder against the wrong building?

I don't know how many times I have watched myself and others do things for the wrong audience. The truth is this: The audience you perform for reflects the approval you seek. If you were invited by the President to the White House to receive a lifetime achievement award, and you had a five-person table at the banquet, whose names would you turn in, living or dead? That will tell you who is in the audience you are performing for. For some, it's a mother or father who never showed them love. For others, it might be friends or business peers.

But the Lord has changed the audience for this old football player. I see my heavenly Father there. And I see His Son. Sure, there are some people I would love to have there, but I know that ultimately it's what God thinks that really matters and grows us into the person He has called us to become.

It's the same with your kids. Are they living under the smile of their Father in heaven? To get there, they first must have your smile. If they don't see dad's smile, it's much harder to connect with the one who is smiling from above.

Children who don't know the smile of their fathers have a hard time hearing God's call for their lives. They don't know how to make sacrifices, take risks, and obtain all that their dreams entail. But you can change the destiny of your children's lives by instilling those truths in them. You can make a difference in their lives that is true and lasting. So, how do we do that?

For Chapter Four study guide and questions, visit: www.thedifferenceafathermakes.com

CHAPTER FIVE

Building God's Smile over Your Kids

So, how do you build God's smile over your kids? It first begins with you! It is true that things are more caught than taught. When I found His smile for me, it was an easy transition to speak to my kids the way the Father was speaking to me. When I discovered that God's heart toward me was so full of joy and blessing that He actually rejoices over me, it changed the way I prayed, read my Bible, and worshipped. It even gave me a different perspective when I entered difficult times in life. Understanding the Father's heart toward you changes the way you live.

1 John 4:19 says, *"We love because He first loved us."* When my heart is filled with His love for me, it opens me to love my wife and my kids with such passion that I know it couldn't possibly originate from me. That is where

you start to build the environment that paints God's smile over their lives. When you love someone with all your heart, what do you want to do for them? You want to bless them. That's our starting point.

The blessing

When you bless something or someone, it gives them permission to move forward. How many times have you seen someone paralyzed by life because he doesn't know who he is or what he is here for? You can see what his or her life could be, but their view of their identity is masked by the question, "Who am I?" I have to come to realize the powerful responsibility God places in every man who fathers children. It is the power of blessing.

I have a friend who ministers to prisoners, and he asks every inmate the same question: "Did your father ever tell you that you would end up in prison?" He told me that most of the inmates he asks this question say their fathers told them that prison was in their future. Our words are powerful instruments. Consider what James wrote:

Now if we put the bits into the horses' mouths so that they will obey us, we direct their entire body as well. Look at the ships also, though they are so great and are driven by strong winds, are still directed by a very small rudder wherever the inclination of the pilot desires. So also the tongue is a small part of the body, and yet it boasts of great things. See how great a forest is set aflame by such a small fire!

— James 3:3-5

In other words, a small rudder for the life of your children in the hands of a skilled father can set a course for the direction of their future. A word of blessing enables your kids to believe that their dad believes in them. Did you have a father who spoke blessings over your life?

When you declare your heart over your children, you cement God's smile over their future. This blessing announces that a new season is beginning — the old way of just being a little girl or boy has ended, and now they are ready to face the challenges and dreams of their next chapter in life.

Calling out our kids doesn't mean that their race is over or that they have reached maturity. The act of calling them out is more about giving affirmative permission that they are now ready for the challenges ahead. Let me share with you about the passage of my daughter Mary.

Mary's passage

Mary is my dancer, ballerina, actress, and beauty queen all rolled into one. For several years, Mary heard Jessica's story of being called into womanhood and experienced some jealousy. She kept asking, "Dad, when am I going to become a woman?" Mary knew that her life was going to change when she became a woman. Mary had watched the transformation in her older brother and sister. She said, "When I become a woman, I will have more responsibility. I will be respected. I will be heard. I will no longer be treated as a little girl. I am also excited about the ring because it will be a symbol of who has my heart, and I want my friends to see that."

At first Mary asked monthly, and then the frequency increased to weekly. As the date crept to within 10 weeks, she began a daily countdown. I prayed about it and felt like her 14th birthday would be the appropriate time for her "ceremony."

Finally, the ring was purchased and the night came. I had selected a special ring made in Ireland, depicting two hands holding a heart. The restaurant we chose, Mr. Stocks, was known for preparing some of the best steaks in town. After two hours of preparation, Mary walked out of the bathroom with her hair done up and a beautiful new dress. "Wow!" I said. She just took my breath away!

You know that moment when your "Little House on the Prairie" girl becomes a "diva"? She was stunning. "Behold the woman!" I exclaimed. My daughter was now ending her season as a little girl, transitioning into the first chapter of her adult identity.

Mary, taking my arm as we walked to the car, said, "Daddy, a woman needs to have her car door opened. A gentleman always opens the door for a lady." My wife just loves the training my daughters are giving me!

We arrived at the restaurant and walked down the long hallway toward the front door. I was envisioning a time in the future when I would walk Mary down another aisle, giving her away to the man of God's choosing. The waiter greeted us and we sat down at a special table in the back of the restaurant. Mary could hardly contain herself; she was restless and excited, shifting from side to side in her chair. I started her rite of passage by telling her all the things I love about her.

Here are just a few:

I looked into her eyes and said, "Since the day you were born I have known that God has special plans for you. God has made you beautiful, both on the inside and outside. I love your heart, Mary. Every time you walk into a room, you light it up. You have repeatedly shown an amazing ability to reach out and care for others, often at the expense of your own needs. You give a hug to every-

one you meet and say, 'Hi, I'm Mary! It is good to meet you!' I can't tell you how many times you have approached me and given me a big kiss, and said 'I love you, Daddy.'

"You light up my life, Mary!

"Not only are you beautiful and have a loving spirit, but God has also given you a beautiful mind. You are one of the smartest people I know, and I love the way you do everything with all your heart. Except for your bedroom! The reports from your school have blown me away. You are so far ahead of my best work when I was your age. I am so proud of you.

"You just love adventure. I love the stories you tell when you and Alana come back from journeys. You are either sharing the love of Jesus with other people, meeting the most interesting people in the world, or finding pirate treasure in the cliffs. Mary, God has put His favor on your life; He has an amazing adventure awaiting you."

As I thought about the love I have for my Mary, it was hard to hold back the tears. I have learned that I am most fully alive as a man and father when I give myself permission to pour my heart out to my children. All I can tell you is that my Father in heaven has irrevocably injected my heart with His love for my kids.

I continued to share my heart with Mary:

"I also love the respect and care you show your friends — the way you love and serve them. Your heart is so tender that sometimes

you are easily wounded. We are alike in that way. ...

"When you found out there was not a Christian club in your junior high school, you went to the principal and asked permission to start one. You and your friends started meeting and sharing your faith. When you didn't have answers for them, you would come home in the evenings and ask questions so you would have something useful to say to them. I also love your boldness. You are never afraid to stand up and speak the truth. ...

"You are, and will always be, my Princess. I remember you as a little girl putting on a cone princess hat with a trailing ribbon, and running back and forth in front of my office to get my attention."

After about half an hour of affirming and complimenting her, I shared with Mary the biblical example of a righteous woman, taking my cue from Proverbs 31.

I then reached into my pocket and pulled out the ring. I held her hand and began to slip the ring onto her finger as I said, "Mary, I give this ring to you because I love you. I want you to know that this ring is a token of your commitment between you, me, and God — that you will hold back your physical body from any boy until the day you give this ring to your husband at the altar. Will you do that?" Her eyes were filled with tears. She said, "Yes, Daddy, I will." I finished slipping the ring on her finger and said, "Mary, from this point on, you are no longer a little girl; you are a woman."

She leapt across the side of the table and gave me the sweetest embrace a father could receive from his daughter — much like the embrace I will receive the day I walk her down the aisle and give her to her future husband.

Giving permission

I cannot tell you how many young people I have met who have never received permission to move into the next stage of their lives. A big part of what happens during a rite of passage is that the father is calling the child out into an adult relationship with God as well as into an adult relationship with his or her parents. This permission moves them into their next season where they will no longer be fundamentally accountable to their parents alone, but accountable in their own relationship with God. They will no longer look primarily to daddy for acceptance and validation. Your smile merely anchors them into their heavenly Father's relentless tenderness and pursuit. I love the way C.S. Lewis described the pursuit of the Father.

> The steady unrelented approach of
> Him whom I so earnestly desired not to
> meet. ... I never had the experience of look-

ing for God. It was the other way around.
He was the hunter and I was the deer. He
stalked me like a redskin, took unerring aim,
and fired.

This permission is so important because it helps
them move away from an adolescent identity that is largely
defined by their resistance to their parents' imposed
morals, expectations, and behav-
ioral standards. It moves them
closer to discovering who they are
based on their true identity as a
beloved son or daughter of God.
Missing this step with teenagers
can make the already difficult adolescent years even more difficult!
For me, it was like a light bulb
went off in my heart when I realized my son didn't hate me; he
simply wanted permission to be
his own man. That was a great day in the McGlasson
household!

> For me, it was like a light bulb went off in my heart when I realized my son didn't hate me; he simply wanted permission to be his own man.

The promises they're making (of chastity, honesty,
health choices, etc.) aren't really to their dad, but to their
heavenly Father, in a new, more vital, more direct, and
more adult relationship. Part of "the timing is right for

this rite" is that we have sensed that the adolescent is already motivated to move into a more mature adult relationship with God — their ultimate Father. Your affirmative permission gives them the courage to walk out this commitment. I have watched my own kids move from playtime to a healthy self-awareness about their unique gifts and calling.

Without this permission many young people are propelled into life motivated by toys and diversions, like the bumper sticker I saw on an RV that had a speedboat in tow, two dirt bikes mounted on the trailer, and assorted recreational products strapped to the roof. It read, "The man with the most toys at the end of the game wins." That's not what I want to motivate my kids throughout their adult lives!

What commitments are you encouraging your kids to make? Who are you giving your children permission to be?

Releasing confidence

Blessing your kids and naming the potential greatness you see in them empowers them to understand that they have been uniquely made for a purpose. It links directly to their self-image and confidence. Remember how awkward you felt in your body when your teenage years started? Your body was changing. Girls stopped having "cooties." Girls' bodies started to make you nervous. Not having the voice of a father in the home makes this time even more confusing. The tradition of bar mitzvah seems to be divinely timed, at the age of 13, doesn't it? How many young people have you seen lose their futures to the wrong crowd? If ever there is a developmental stage that needs the stabilizing voice of a loving father, it is during this time.

The pressure our little girls have to deal with in high school — friends who have developed faster, a bombardment of sensual images from the media, the raging hormones of teenage boys — can drive a dad crazy. I discovered something by accident about the effects of dating my daughter. The combination of the blessing I gave them and learning how to be consistently affectionate released a healthy body consciousness in my girls. It gave them a greater confidence in who they are and the way they look. A friend of mine once said, "Confidence is the byproduct of predictability." When your daughters know what daddy thinks, the confidence produced can empower them to hold off the sexual mores of this culture. In other words, they can say "no" and mean it. When you know who you are and what you're for, you can say "yes" and "no" with confidence. My wife taught me that my daughters' views of their own bodies are directly related to my showing affection toward them. My dates with my girls have done much more than I ever would have guessed. Our girls still will have to make their own choices in the future, but I think that giving them the right foundation will equip them to ward off the approaches of a "pretender."

Building trust

The blessing also changes the nature of the way you relate to your kids. Up to the time of the teenage years, most parenting happens from the top down. The majority of training is about your rules and the way you want them to behave. Have you learned, like I have, that the prisoners want to be released?

I wish I could tell you I moved into my new role easily. There were times when you could see steam rising off of my head when my rules were not followed; only later did I understand that my usual style of leadership wasn't working anymore. Most of the parent-teenager problems I deal with come from parents trying to use the same hammer on their teenager that worked when they were younger.

I hear things from teenagers like, "I want my dad to respect me and trust me" or "I want to have my own space." Developmentally, their journey into adulthood begins in their hearts and bodies long before they are able to understand what is happening inside them. Teenagers want to be respected and trusted for their decisions. Learning not to give advice until they ask for it, letting them suggest their own rules, and moving from parent to coach sometimes stretched me past the edges of my ability. Learning not to give the answer before they were asking for it — that was a hard one! My number one prayer during that time was, *"Help me, God, before I go crazy!"*

When you begin to treat your children like adults, it communicates to them that you trust them and feel that they have a voice that matters. Your trust in them calls out the song God put in their hearts.

But where does accountability fit into the picture? Giving away power to kids is scary for parents. The truth is that if you don't release them to their next season, they are not going to obey your rules anyway. You might see them perform in front of you; but in the end, they are only going to follow their own rules when they are with their friends.

When your children have their own voice in defining their own standards and rules, the issue of accountability becomes much easier to handle. When they begin breaking the rules they created, the questions about accountability are pretty clear.

Mary's passage, part two

Our waitress had crept up to our table and was watching from a distance. The waitress looked into Mary's tear-swollen eyes and asked, "Are you OK?"

My daughter looked up and said, "Yes!"

"Then why are you crying?" the waitress asked.

Mary replied, "I just became a woman!"

With an incredulous look, the waitress asked, "What, you became a what?"

"A woman," Mary responded. "I just became a woman. My dad brought me here tonight to teach me what a woman is — to tell me that I am no longer a little girl but a woman. He wanted to tell me that he loves me and believes in me."

The waitress continued to ask both of us questions about what had just occurred. She made a statement I have heard so many times. "I wish my dad had done this with me. I think my life would have been different than it is. I have had so many heartbreaks, and the relationship I am in is almost over." Her eyes were swelling as she tried to hold back the tears. Mary and I reached out to this young woman and asked if we could pray for her. I watched my new adult daughter put her hands on this 35-year-old woman and ask the Father to bless her life. She pushed back her tears and told us that we had made her night.

That waitress was a blessing sent from God to Mary that night. It marked the beginning of my daughter's adult life. Mary later told me that, when she became a woman that evening, she started to realize what an honor it meant to be "the kind of woman who lives for God and makes a difference." When Mary verbalized to the waitress what had just happened to her, I watched the things I had just called out come alive in her. To be able to say with certainty, "I just became a woman," further solidified what just happened to Mary.

I've found that this little ritual — this celebration of my children's uniqueness and of my recognition of their growing adult identity — anchors them in a foundation of self-acceptance that is transformational. Not only do they know who they are, but they know with certainty that their daddy knows and deeply values them.

My daughters have friends whose fathers don't understand this truth or even know what to do. Starved for their dad's affection and recognition, they seek out a boy to try and fill this need. I've spoken with many young women who have become involved in illicit and unhealthy relationships with boys because their fathers did not know how to express their affection for them.

However, there is no foolproof solution. Sometimes a daughter can be shown large amounts of affection — her dad does everything "right" — and yet she may still choose to make unhealthy choices. Our job is to build the foundation; theirs is to build the house. I wish I could say that this is a magic formula, but raising kids is more art than science. Being willing to improvise in the moment, based on the guiding power of the Holy Spirit, will bring you home.

What do you think the term "woman" means to your daughter? The answer to that question may surprise you. The answer is modeled in the way you love your wife — how you date her, speak to her, and celebrate her. It defines in your daughter's mind what becoming a woman really means. The phrase "you are a woman," means little if you have not modeled it through loving her mom.

Remember that moms want to be dated, cuddled, cherished, and honored. Our children learn the most from us by what we do, not what we say.

I love the lyrics from the song *The Best Day of My Life* by George Strait. This song tells the story of a father and his son on the son's wedding day.

> *Standing in a little room*
> *Back of the church with our tuxes on*
> *Looking at him I say I can't believe son that you're grown*

He said Dad
This could be the best day of my life
I've been dreaming day and night
Of being like you
Now its me and her
Watching you and mom I've learned
I'm the luckiest man alive
This is the best day of my life

"Watching you and mom, I've learned." What a great line! One of the greatest gifts you can give your kids is to extravagantly love your wife.

I know that some of you reading this are no longer living with your wife. I don't write these words to shame you; but even after divorce, a father can make a difference — even if you have been separated by the walls of the courts or by distance. What if you're physically or emotionally disconnected from your kids right now? Divorce, addictions, and adrenaline lifestyles have separated many dads from their kids. Now is the day to start making a difference. I have watched countless dads come to terms with the shame they have felt about their inability to make their marriage work, or even the pain they caused their own children. But they took a stand and won their kids' hearts back.

There was a man in my church who hadn't seen his son in over 20 years. His attempts to reconnect were rejected. As he talked about his son, his eyes swelled with tears. His story is a common one: a bitter divorce, hurt and anger on both sides, and his son taking a stand with mom by telling his dad that he didn't want to talk to him ever again. This experience left this father feeling hopeless that he could ever make a difference in his son's life.

We joined hands that day and asked God to change his son's heart. I encouraged him to write his son a letter and tell him that he has missed him, and how much he wanted to reconnect.

"I will try," he said, "but he will probably never respond." His son called him the week he got the letter and said, "Dad, I didn't think you wanted me. When you divorced mom, I thought it was because you didn't want me, and your silence all these years further reinforced my assumptions about what you thought of me."

After a tearful talk on the phone, they made arrangements to meet. You should have been there when this restored father returned from his trip. "We spent most of the time crying and asking each other for forgiveness," he told me. The crowning moment was when he held his grandchildren for the first time. It shattered that papa! He told me that his own father was never able to

mouth the words, "Son, I love you" or "I believe in you."
He never had a role model to teach him how to be verbal-
ly and physically generous with his kids. His restoration
with his son evoked all the emotional and physical
responses he had always wanted to express. His heart had
called him to action, and, in the end, love means little
when it's not embedded in action.

This book doesn't come from a fellow dad who has
all the answers, but from a guy, like you, who caught a
message from heaven, a message on how we can recreate
in the lives of our own kids the kind of "developmental
baptism" that the Father gave Jesus at the start of His
adulthood. I am sold out to learning how to love my children like the Father loved Jesus. By blessing my children, I
release them into their God-given birthright that produces
healthy self-confidence, boldness, and productivity that He
desires for them.

After reading what I've tried to do with my kids,
what are some things you might do to honor and celebrate
your kids? What can you do that will launch them success-
fully on the path of confidence, wholeness, and stability?
How might you make a current and bold difference in the
lives of your kids?

For Chapter Five study guide and questions,
visit: www.thedifferenceafathermakes.com

CHAPTER SIX

X's & O's: Your Playbook to Make a Difference

L et's explore some principles we have learned about helping kids transition effectively from adolescence into adulthood. See what thoughts or images arise in your mind about your relationship with your own kids as we review them.

1. Fill your children with positive affirmations.

What is the one thing that you wanted most from your own dad or stepfather? I know what I wanted. I wanted him to be proud of me as his son. Wasn't that what you hoped for?

There is a 20-something single mom in our church whose life recently began a quick free fall. She lost her job, her car, and couldn't pay her bills. Everything around her was crumbling. She stated, "I have tried to do everything I know to do, but it's all just falling apart."

After hearing her story, I asked if her father had ever told her that he believed in her — if he ever affirmed her and told her what he loved about the person she was. She immediately started crying.

"No," she responded. "The other day when you told the church about Mary's special day, I lost it. I had to leave the room because I couldn't stop crying. I have wanted my dad to do that my whole life. But he just wasn't there."

Sensing that this was one of those "God moments," I reached out my hand and asked her if I could pray with her. I told her that the Father in heaven had come today to change her future.

I said to her, "You need to understand something."

"What?" she replied.

"Your Father in heaven wants you to know that He believes in you, and so do I!" I said.

Her tears started pouring out as I continued. "He doesn't see you as a failure. From this moment on, you are no longer a little girl. You are His woman."

Broken by the Father's love, she said, "I have been waiting for this moment all my life. All I have ever wanted is to be loved and cared for."

A few nights later, her mother came up to me and said, "You will never know how much that experience blessed my daughter. I tried to do everything I could for her as a single mom, but she needed a dad to speak into her life and believe in her. Your words met a need inside of her she has had her whole adult life. My daughter didn't stop crying for two days."

Over the past few years, God has brought me boys, girls, men and women from ages 12 to 78 years old who were still looking for the affirmation their fathers never gave them.

A 78-year-old business man came up to me with tears in his eyes after one of my conferences in Denver and said, "Ed, today you answered a question I have waited 62 years to have answered. I thought if I worked hard enough and made enough money, my dad would approve of me. But now I have a Father in heaven who calls me His beloved."

Think about the people you love hanging around. Are they the ones who spend their time building you up or tearing you down? Are they people who are preoccupied with themselves — with their own challenges and opportunities — or are they the people who see and publicly honor the best things in you, the gifts and intentions that you even lose sight of at times? The most powerful four word sentence that can be spoken over someone's life is, "I believe in you!"

Recently, I was at the driving range watching my son

practice. One of his teammates came by to hit golf balls with him. He asked me if I could help him as well. I spent some time encouraging him and loving him. I reflected back to him some of the great things I saw in his golf swing and that I had seen in previous interactions between him and his friends. I told him I believed in him. He looked at me and said, "I wish you could be my dad. You are always around, supporting your son, but my dad has never even seen me play golf."

My heart sank! What a treasure that dad was missing. Instead of participating in his son's life in a way that would have been unbelievably fulfilling for both of them, he was spending his life working to support his perfect Orange County home, missing the experience of being a father who makes a difference.

Affirmation is not rocket science. We dramatically underestimate the importance of a father's validation. We find ourselves focusing more on what's imperfect in our kids than promoting our appreciation of who they are and who they can become.

I remember walking off the field following my last high school football game. We had been severely trounced that day. Standing on the sideline was my stepfather, with the biggest smile I had ever seen on his face. His words still ring in my ears. "Heckuva game, son! You kicked some serious butt today!" I can feel the effect that bit of recognition had on me even today.

Your father's heart

In the space provided below, answer this question: What are five things you love about your son or daughter? It is probably easier to write down the top five things that drive you crazy, or the five things you wish you could fix in them. How about what you most love about them? Or what about the great things you see in them?

1.

2.

3.

4.

5.

What action could you take today, dad, to affirm those things in your son or daughter? How might you make a difference, today?

It's time to connect! Give them a call, give them a boisterous hug, take them out to dinner, or write them a note.

Make a commitment to yourself and to God that from this day forward, "I am going to spend myself loving and affirming my kids, or whatever disconnected boys or girls God brings to me. I am going to be a loving, generative father to both my natural kids and to whoever else God brings my way!"

2. Bless your children publicly.

Not only do your children need positive affirmation, they need it to be done in public. Positive public affirmation is a way of showing them what you feel. Public affirmation cements your words deep in their hearts. God the Father spoke publicly over the life of Jesus at the Jordan River. That is our model and task as fathers — to speak publicly and affirmatively over our kids.

On another occasion, God again spoke those same words over Jesus. Peter wrote, *"For when He received honor and glory from God the Father, such an utterance as this was made*

to Him by the Majestic Glory, "This is My beloved Son with whom I am well-pleased" — and we ourselves heard this utterance made from heaven when we were with Him on the holy mountain"
(2 Peter 1:17-18).

Do you think those disciples who were present had any further doubt concerning whether Jesus was really God's Son or how the Father felt about Him? I love the way the Message translation states it: *"This is my Son, marked by my love, focus of all my delight."*

Do your kids believe they are the focus of your delight? Do the rest of your family members and your friends know what you see in your kids?

There may be nothing more meaningful to your children than hearing you talk lovingly about them in the presence of their peers.

At my conferences, I occasionally set up a wall of honor where the fathers stand on one side of the room and the boys who are waiting to be called out stand on the other side. One by one, young men wait for their father's words. There is a moment when the father moves forward to begin to publicly calling out his son. Without fail, there is not a dry eye in the house as the son crumbles under the affirming words of his father or mentor. Sometimes those celebrations of passage have lasted three hours. I know that for some of the dads, it is the first time they have publicly affirmed their sons.

Another option is to take your son away on a weekend with five or six other men who know and love him. You might ask your son whom he respects as a man, and have him invite them to be present. At some designated point during the weekend, speak the kind of deep affirmation into your son's life that you long to give and that he longs to hear. Have the other men do the same thing. It is important to understand that it is not the ceremony but the words and actions of men who know and love your son which have a transformational impact.

Sons want to know where the goal line is. Someone has to tell them when they have "arrived." When those words come from a father, something powerful happens.

Adding grandma and grandpa to the mix can make the event even more powerful. A dear friend of mine had the ceremony for his two sons on the day they graduated from high school. He invited the most significant people in his son's life, along with grandma and grandpa. One by one, grandpa, grandma, younger brother, older brother, and then mom and dad read a letter of blessing they had prepared beforehand. Every letter started like this: "I hope I can get through this without crying. This is what I think about you..." The tears started no matter how tough the reader was because we are never more like our Father in heaven than when we publicly bless those we love. Try it. It will make a wreck of your adult, emotionless veneer.

Remember the story of Derek Redman, whose father carried him across the finish line at the Olympics? It was a moment that changed both their lives, and has since affected thousands of people worldwide. The same kind of commitment on your part will enable your children to become everything God has called them to be.

3. Develop traditions that highlight shared values and commitments.

Another rite of passage exercise is to give your child a token that will help him remember his or her commitment. For my daughters, I chose a ring similar to my wedding ring which reminds us both of the day I promised to give my heart to only one woman. I gave my son a memento that means something equally powerful to him.

If you choose to go away for a rite of passage weekend with a group of friends, have them bring something they value that would have a message embedded in it. For example, I was asked by my friend, James Ryle, to participate with him in a rite of passage for his son, Jonathan. He asked me to bring a token that his son would never forget. I went to my closet and found a football that was given to me after we beat the Dallas Cowboys in overtime to get to the playoffs. I took the air out of the ball to create a symbolic message.

When it came time for me to do my part, I said, "Jonathan, I am giving you this ball because your life is going to count and because you are a winner. It is out of air because it needs to be filled with faith. I see that in you, Jonathan. I see the heart of courage you have. I believe in you, Jonathan. When you give yourself wholeheartedly to trusting and living by faith, this ball, like your life, is going to be filled. And like this ball, a life filled with faith changes the world."

As a matter of fact, Jonathan's father was the first person I knew who held a rite of passage exercise with his kids. I am grateful for his insight and how he modeled the impact a loving father can have on a child.

My daughters still wear their rings to this day. With all of the temptations our kids have to face, a fully present and praying father makes a big difference. Pray for your children to be protected against sexual temptations thrown at them by the enemy. Commit to walking through these challenges with them in a way that helps them to make it to the finish line as victors.

4. Spend time with your children.

This is where the real commitment begins. Words

are important, but they only frame part of the commitment you are making to your kids.

For my son Edward, spending time meant waking up many mornings at 5:00 a.m. and driving him to the golf course to practice. I hope one day he will be a force that Tiger Woods will have to reckon with. Edward's personal dream needed a dad who would get up in the morning and watch him hit putts, not to mention carrying his bag and caddying for him. I had to make time to be physically and emotionally present with him. There are trade-offs when giving your kids time. It is worth it.

Each one of your treasures has different needs. Here is a little jewel I learned from my kids: Don't assume you know what they need. Ask them how they want you to support them. My assumptions about what they needed often didn't jive with what they really wanted from me.

5. Build structure around your children.

Every dream needs a structure that will sustain it. Otherwise, dreams will die as a mere fantasy. Edward and I set aside a day in which we talked about his future and his dream. We called it a "dream day."

We shaped the day around where he wanted to be in 10 years with both his education and his golf career. I then asked the question, "What is it that you need from me? What are some of the ways I can serve you?" Your kids will not be short of words when they get to tell you what they want.

With pen in hand, we built a plan together. Articulate shared commitments. A penned plan has power. It will keep you on track and facilitate accountability.

Edward and I have revisited that plan and structure many times since. Dream days are a great way to refocus a discouraged young adult in the midst of his dream storms.

There are many ways to build a plan, to build structure. My suggestion is learn how to ask great questions. Asking encourages your kids to build a critical thinking process that will sustain them throughout their lives. Sometimes the best thing to do is let them wrestle with where they are supposed to go, and not give them an easy answer. Remember that a personally discovered truth is much more powerful than one imposed from the outside. When they uncover it for themselves, it ignites a fire in their bellies that you will not be able to extinguish.

6. Celebrate over your children.

How do your kids know when they've crossed the goal line? Who's going to tell them that they've made it, that they are winners?

First, who establishes the goal line? For many, the

goal line is defined by the world's standards. We often define "great men" and "great women" by their accomplishments — the challenges they have faced down, the mountains they've conquered, the hides they've nailed to the wall. Are those the measurements that matter?

Everyone needs to feel like a winner. When the apostle Paul wrote the words, "I have finished my race," he communicated that he knew what the finish line meant. It is possible for your son or daughter to become something bigger than they ever dreamed because they have an involved and affirming dad.

I remember watching Tiger Woods and his dad embrace after he won his first Masters at a golf club that used to discriminate against African-Americans. I cried along with everyone else when I heard Tiger exclaim, "Daddy, we did it!" Those are the moments that inspire us and remind us of the great joys that accompany authentic fatherhood. It may not be a Masters' victory for your child, but there are specific victories throughout each child's life that can and should be celebrated.

The celebration that day for Tiger was surely about the Masters' win. But, more deeply, it was also about the journey that he and his dad had taken together. It expresses the relationship we need with each other, and with our Father to become all we are called to be. John explains our relationship with God this way:

> *See how great a love the Father has bestowed on us, that we would be called children of God; and such we are.*
>
> — *1 John 3:1a*

Have you ever wondered about the intensity of the Father's love for you? Like I mentioned earlier, in Jesus' final prayer before the cross, he prayed to God the Father, *"I have made Your name known to them, and will make it known, so that the love with which You loved Me may be in them, and I in them"* (John 17:26). In other words, Jesus came to give us the same life He experienced, a life lived out of the awareness of being totally and completely loved by His Father. Jesus came to bring us the same relationship He had with His Father.

One afternoon while sitting in my office, I experienced a taste of what the Father in heaven feels about us. My son, Edward, was playing in his first major amateur golf tournament. I was closely watching Edward's scores as they were posted on the Internet. As I watched the scores come in, the intensity of my love for him started welling up in my heart and I found myself dancing around my office! Filled with so much joy, I heard myself shouting and singing over him. Is there anything sweeter than giving yourself over to seeing others win in life?

That is the treasure we have waiting for us as fathers — the dancing-feet joy that comes from releasing all of who we are to making a difference in the lives of our kids and others God brings to our care. It's one way we connect the small, local story of our lives with His larger story.

I was the ultimate "armchair" golf fan that day. I was singing, shouting, and rooting for Edward, even though he was 3,000 miles away on the East Coast. I was so excited that I lost track of time, consumed with the joy of the moment. Realizing I was 45 minutes late for a meeting, I rushed out the door. As I was driving to my meeting, I had an overwhelming love in my heart for Edward, and Zephaniah 3:17 returned to my mind: *"He will rejoice over you with shouts of joy."*

Do you hear the shouts of joy your heavenly Father is proclaiming over you right now?

When did your kids last hear your shouts of rejoicing over them? When you are so excited about the love you have for your child, rejoice! Let it ring out!

For Chapter Six study guide and questions, visit: www.thedifferenceafathermakes.com

The Call

How did I do, Dad? My friend, Dan Paxton, shared an incredible story about a young boy he coached on a high school football team. As Dan's team was finally putting together the pieces of a championship team, they had to beat their rivals to win the conference championship. The day of the game, the skies opened up and dumped buckets of water onto the field. As game time approached, the rain continued pelting the surface so that the field was a virtual mud pit.

Late in the first half of a scoreless game, Dan decided to get tricky and called a pass play in the terrible weather. When the quarterback released the ball, it went straight up in the air and landed in the arms of a defensive lineman, who rumbled into the end zone for a touchdown.

Trailing 6-0 late in the fourth quarter, Dan's team began to put together its first serious scoring threat of the game. As the squad began to move the ball down the field, Dan felt a tug on his coat. When he turned to see who was tugging at him, he saw one of the scrawniest players on his team. Barely five feet tall and 100 pounds, Billy was demanding his coach's attention.

"What do you want?" Dan asked.

"Coach, I want to play," Billy answered.

"Get back on the sideline," Dan said.

As the team drove down to around the 25-yard line, Dan felt another tug on his coat.

"What?" Dan asked again. "Coach, I want to play," Billy said.

"Please go back over to the sideline," Dan said.

Then with the team nearing the 15-yard line, Dan felt yet another pull on his coat. He spun around and saw it was Billy again.

"What is up with you?" Dan said.

"Coach, my parents divorced a few years ago and I haven't seen my dad in five years," Billy said. "He flew in tonight and wants to see me play. I've got to play, Coach."

"What position do you play?" Dan asked.

"I don't care," Billy said.

So Dan instructed Billy to go into the huddle and

send one of the players to the sideline for one play.

As Dan was conferring with one of his assistants on the sideline about which play they should run, he looked up only to see his starting quarterback trotting off the field. Dan was shocked, begging the referees for a time-out, but it was too late.

Somehow, Billy called a play and got underneath center to receive the snap. When the center snapped the ball, it popped Billy in his face mask and fell to the ground. In the mad dash for the fumble, the defense converged upon Billy and the ball hydroplaned out of the pile and right to the team's fullback. He then collected the ball and ran into the end zone for the touchdown.

A jubilant Billy headed for the sideline with his hands raised, yelling, "How did I do?"

"*How did you do?*" Dan thought.

Dan was still in shock from what had just happened; yet he remained unhappy with Billy's decision which could have cost his team the game. With mixed emotions, Dan was ready to answer Billy's question when he looked into his eyes and saw Billy was looking over him and into the stands. As Dan turned around and looked at the crowd, he saw Billy's dad standing and exulting, "You did great, son! You did great!"

"How did I do, Dad?" You see, Billy was not playing

for the approval or validation of the coach; he was playing for his dad. All he wanted to know was, "What does my dad think of me?" Isn't that what you wanted when you were younger? Don't you want that still? How differently would your life look if you knew in your bones that your heavenly Father feels such a joy and tenderness for you that He can't stop dancing?

What kind of father will you be?

Think about that question. What is the nature of the gap between how you've been functioning as a father, and the job you'd like to be doing? I know your heart. I know the yearning you feel to play a vital role, rather than a peripheral role, in your kids' lives. Now is the time to slow down long enough to honestly assess whether or not you are living out the love and commitment that you feel in your heart.

I was recently in Starbucks having my usual afternoon coffee, and was reminiscing about my kids when they were little. Jill would be in the kitchen when the sound of my car pulling up would trigger a response that snapped my kids out of their afternoon play.

It was, "Daddy's home!"

One by one my kids would run out to greet me. With shouts of "Daddy! Daddy!" My boys would fly headfirst into me. I still remember them squeezing my legs with all their might. My girls came next to kiss and hug me, saying, "Do you love me, Daddy?" I would respond, "I do, with all my heart." Is there anything sweeter than the loving embrace of your kids? My young Jessica used to say, "Daddy, I love you too much!"

One of the reasons I wrote this book is to restore the festive shout in every home across the world that "Daddy's home! And I can't wait to be with him!"

Will you join me and make a decision to add your home to the list of those where the voice of the father truly lives? It is part of your destiny as a man to love your kids with all your heart and to help launch them into their adult years in the same way that the heavenly Father launched Jesus into His adult ministry. One of the highest purposes of a man is be a generous father.

Many years ago, I was challenged by a story in the Bible that confronted me with that very question: "What kind of father will I be?" In the story of David and Goliath, King Saul was watching from a distance and saw something about David that moved his heart:

As Saul watched David going out to meet the Philistine, he said to Abner, commander of the army, "Abner, whose son is that young man?" Abner replied, "As surely as you live, O king, I don't know." The king said, "Find out whose son this young man is." As soon as David returned from killing the Philistine, Abner took him and brought him before Saul, with David still holding the Philistine's head. "Whose son are you, young man?" Saul asked him. David said, "I am the son of your servant Jesse of Bethlehem."

— 1 Samuel 17:55-58 (NIV)

Saul was really saying, "I want to meet the father who raised a son like this! I want to meet the man who turned this shepherd boy into the man of courage, trust and confidence that he is today. I want to meet that man!"

I remember thinking, "I want to be that kind of father."

How about you? What kind of father will you be?

Coming Fall 2007!

Be-Loved
Embracing God's unconditional love and acceptance
by Ed Tandy McGlasson

Don't miss Ed McGlasson's follow-up book to *The Difference a Father Makes* where he addresses the struggle that almost every man and woman faces in their lives: trying to earn God's approval and love. In fact, it's a never-ending battle for many people, who strive to win the love of Father God. The problem is, it's impossible because we already have it ... we must simply learn to embrace it. When we begin living under the smile of the Father, embracing His love and approval, our worlds are turned upside down. The way you relate to God, your family and your friends will forever be changed as these truths will transform your heart!

Sign up for new release announcements at:
www.ampelonpublishing.com

about the author

Ed Tandy McGlasson, a former lineman in the National Football League for a handful of teams, pastors the Stadium Vineyard in Anaheim, California. After getting healed from a knee injury that led to his conversion, Ed eventually entered the ministry after another knee injury ended his NFL career. He has spoken at numerous conferences across the country and around the world. Ed and his wife, Jill, live in Anaheim with their five children.

If you would like to contact him to speak or just to drop him a note, you may do so by visiting the book's website at: www.thedifferenceafathermakes.com

your story

I want to hear your story! Share with other men the difference you have been able to make in the lives of your children. Go to this book's website:

www.thedifferenceafathermakes.com

At the website, you'll be able to post your stories and testimonials, read inspiring stories about fathering from other dads, sign up for a newsletter, and download additional resources that will help you on your journey.

ampelon publishing

*Resourcing the local church,
refreshing hearts and souls*

www.ampelonpublishing.com

other ampelon publishing titles

God's Relentless Pursuit: Discovering His Heart for Humanity
by Phil Strout
retail price: $10.95

Have you ever considered that instead of us chasing God, He is actually the one chasing us? In this book, discover God's mission on earth and how His people join in His mission: to draw people into relationship with Him. Many common ideas and notions regarding our role in pursuing God are challenged as we discover the truth about what God is doing in and around us, both across the street and across the oceans.

Rediscovering the Power of Repentance & Forgiveness
by Dr. Leah Coulter
retail price: $12.95

There is something deep within the heart of every man and woman that longs to see justice prevail. But what about when injustices are committed against us? How do we move forward? Can we really just forgive and forget?

Through a thorough examination of biblical teaching on forgiveness within the context of ancient Jewish culture, Dr. Leah Coulter dispels the notion that forgiveness is a one-way street. She explains the true depth of forgiveness and the freedom that results in a genuine heart of repentance. With personal stories and other examples, she gives readers a pathway to repentance and forgiveness, as well as showing them how to find healing and justice when they have been wronged by someone who has not repented.

about ampelon publishing

Ampelon Publishing exists to resource the local church, equipping pastors and leaders to raise up committed followers of Christ, and encouraging believers to go deeper in their faith. We are driven by our passion for the message, discovering the relevant words for our time, and communicating them in an effective way.

For more questions, comments, or more information regarding Ampelon Publishing, you may write to us at: Ampelon Publishing, 6920 Jimmy Carter Blvd., Suite 200, Norcross, GA 30071.

You may also visit us on the Internet at our website: www.ampelonpublishing.com